Marianne Moore:
Vision into Verse

Marianne Moore. George Platt Lynes, 1935.

Marianne Moore:
Vision into Verse

by
Patricia C. Willis

The Rosenbach Museum & Library
Philadelphia
1987

This catalogue is published on the occasion of an exhibition held at:

The Rosenbach Museum & Library, Philadelphia
The Joseph Regenstein Library, The University of Chicago
The Grolier Club, New York
The Folger Shakespeare Library, Washington, D.C.

ISBN-0-939084-21-X

Table of Contents

Acknowledgements

This exhibition is the culmination of a long process, and thanks are due to many people who have assisted me, both directly and indirectly, in preparing it. Clive E. Driver, as Director of the Rosenbach Museum & Library in 1969, arranged for the acquisition of the Marianne Moore Collection. His intimate knowledge of the poet's work has been essential in shaping the exhibition. Ellen S. Dunlap has enthusiastically supported the exhibition since becoming Director of the Rosenbach in 1983. Evelyn W. Feldman contributed a full year of research, drawing as well on her many years' work in the Collection; her generous assistance in preparing the exhibition has been indispensable. Carol Jones Neuman aided in preparing the catalogue and in mounting the exhibition. Leslie A. Morris contributed her bibliographer's expertise to the catalogue and Kimerly Rorschach helped with conservation, mounting, and arrangements for transporting the exhibition to other sites. Joan Watson, Elaine Wilner, and Kathleen Edwards arranged for public programs associated with the exhibition. Emily Mitchell Wallace read and commented upon the catalogue essay. Monroe Wheeler, Marianne Moore's lifelong friend and early publisher, offered advice on the design of the catalogue.

Others who have given of their time to explore the collection for materials associated with Marianne Moore's poems are Veronica Bowlan, Louise Collins, Esther Diamondstone, Lynn Henson, Helen Hughitt, and Doreen Newton. The Conservation Center for Art and Historic Artifacts, Philadelphia, has conserved many items in the exhibition.

Thanks are also due to the staffs at the other institutions which will host the exhibition: Robert Rosenthal, Head of Special Collections, and Jeff Abt, Exhibition Designer, The Regenstein Library, The University of Chicago; Robert Nikirk, Librarian, The Grolier Club; and Werner Gundersheimer, Director, The Folger Shakespeare Library.

Acknowledgement is also made to the following for permission to reproduce material in the catalogue:
Arts Magazine, Der Bayerische Stattsgemaldesammlungen, Munich, Rosemary Watt, Keeper of the Burrell Collection, Glasgow, Mrs. John Steuart Curry, The Friends of Prospect Park, Brendan Gill, The Peggy Guggenheim Foundation, The Herzog Anton Ulrich-Museum, Braunschweig, James Laughlin IV, The Macmillan Company, Sir Oliver Miller, Keeper of the Queen's Pictures, The Robert Miller Gallery, The New York City Ballet, The New York Public Library, *The New York Times*, The Port Authority of New York and New Jersey, The Vatican Museum, The Board of Trustees of the Victoria and Albert Museum, and Viking/Penguin, Inc.

And finally, we gratefully acknowledge generous support from the Mabel Pew Myrin Trust (for cataloging of the Moore archive), the National Endowment for the Humanities (for planning), and the Pennsylvania Humanities Council (for exhibit implementation).

P.C.W.

An Original Sensibility

The Development of Marianne Moore as a Modernist Poet

T. S. Eliot, in his introduction to Marianne Moore's *Selected Poems*, writes of his conviction that

Miss Moore's poems form part of the small body of durable poetry written in our time; of that small body of writings, among what passes for poetry, in which an original sensibility and alert intelligence and deep feeling have been engaged in maintaining the life of English language.

William Carlos Williams said in 1948 that hers was

a talent which diminishes the tom-toming on the hollow men of a wasteland to an irrelevant pitter-patter. Nothing is hollow or waste to the imagination of Marianne Moore.

H. D. wrote in *The Egoist* in 1916:

Miss Moore turns her perfect craft as the perfect craftsman must inevitably do, to some direct presentation of beauty, cut in flowing lines, but so delicately that the very screen she carves seems meant to stand only in that serene palace of her own world of inspiration — frail, yet as all beautiful things are, absolutely hard — and destined to endure....

A letter from Ezra Pound in 1918 was filled with his quirky praise:

Now, to be more amiable [he has criticized a poem], have you a book of verse in print? And, if not, can I get one into print for you?... At any rate, I will buy a copy of your book IF it is in print, and if not I want to see a lot of it all together. You will never sell more than five hundred copies, as your work demands mental attention....

Your stuff holds my eye....
Thank God, I think you can be trusted not to pour out flood (in the manner of dear Amy and poor Masters).

Marianne Moore held a place of honor among her contemporaries. Her work was to them important, genuine poetry so different from that of any other poet, that Eliot, long a student of the genre, was forced to admit finding no derivations for it. Her poetry was decidedly modern: patterned but non-accentual, rhymed but not obviously, and embracing subjects as far from conventional poetry as anything later found in Pound's *Cantos* or Williams's *Paterson*. Difficult, at times even obscure, her poetry, so relished by her contemporaries, is only now beginning to receive widespread critical attention.

Broadly, what the record reveals is that, though she developed her relentlessly modern work in relative isolation, Marianne Moore followed the poetry renaissance from its inception in little magazines. With her first publications, she was embraced by a minuscule but vastly important group of admirers — the other modernist poets. And just ten years later, in 1925, she was named editor of *The Dial*, the country's most prestigious magazine of arts and letters. From that position she became arguably the most powerful arbiter of modernist poetry of the decade. She went on to win every prize offered poets in this country and to become the famous poet in the tricorne hat whose work was widely translated — into Italian, French, Spanish, German, Dutch, Polish, even into Arabic.

Marianne Moore's centenary provides an occasion to review this poet's place in the history of modern poetry. The enormous documentation Moore left behind her in her archive at the Rosenbach Museum & Library in Philadelphia makes that task possible. By highlighting here a part of that history — the poet's beginnings and her early prominence among her peers — we can see how the spirit of the modern era shaped her work and how her poetry, in turn, marked the modernist period.

After 1960, the poets who created the "new" verse just before World War I became the subjects of increased academic interest. Marianne Moore received a far smaller share than her male counterparts, though a slightly larger one than the other women. In 1970, books and essays on Eliot outnumbered those on Moore seventy to six while Stevens, Pound, and Williams were each the subject of about twenty. That year, not a single article about H.D. appeared.

All that is changing. 1986 alone saw the publication of three full-length critical studies of Moore and the first appearance of her *Complete Prose*. A new generation of poets has discovered her and her work is increasingly taught in schools and colleges. By the end of her centenary year, both her poems and her prose will wear the bright orange spine of the Penguin book, assuring her work an accessible and permanent place among the classics in English, an appropriate niche for a major modernist poet.

This essay will focus on Moore's development as a modernist poet, examining in detail her early years, her first appearance as a professional poet, and her presence on the modernist literary scene through 1929. While many of her great poems were to follow this period, the die-cutting of the essential Marianne Moore poem took place early. Marianne Moore never alluded to the fact that as a girl she set out to become a poet and worked untiringly toward that goal. Neither did she discuss the fact that her fellow poets accepted her as a modernist poet from the moment that her first poems appeared in the little magazines. However, the testimony to these truths abounds.

The American Modernists

Modernism in poetry has come to mean the work of Ezra Pound, T. S. Eliot, Marianne Moore, Wallace Stevens, Hilda Doolittle, William Carlos Williams, and their near contemporaries. Although it subsumes the cross-currents of the named "isms" of the period — imagism, futurism, cubism, vorticism, dadaism, precisionism, and synchromism among them — modernism is not a term which those writers applied to their own work. The poets we think of as a group did not consider themselves a school nor did they write according to a single aesthetic formula. Rather, they knew themselves to be modern, or of their own time, breaking with traditional poetic conventions. In Pound's words, they would "Make It New."

The roots of modernism are still tangled. While the development of modern painting can be fairly well charted from Cézanne's radical perceptions of light to Picasso's dismemberment of form, that of modernist poetry remains puzzling. Ezra Pound clearly stands out as the prime mover of the change. A new kind of verse is reflected in his poetry, beginning with *Ripostes* in 1912; his role as an agent for change can be seen even more dramatically in his facilitating the publication of others' work. Harriet Shaw Weaver of *The Egoist*, knowing of his connections to unconventional young poets, hired him as poetry editor; Harriet Monroe chose him as her foreign editor for *Poetry*. He promoted the work of Eliot and H. D. while at the same time he explored Japanese Noh dramas with Yeats. From his London base, he spoke out fearlessly for the new poetry. His famous criteria for imagist verse, published in the fourth issue of *Poetry*

(1913), drew the line separating the old from the new. He counseled:

1. Direct treatment of the "thing," whether subjective or objective.
2. To use absolutely no word that does not contribute to the presentation.
3. As regarding rhythm: to compose in sequence of the musical phrase, not in sequence of a metronome.

Although Pound led the battle for change, he and his troops were the American products of an era when Tennyson reigned as laureate and Whitman remained unsung. We know what the modernists created; we know less about what created them.

The American modernist poets were all born within the decade beginning in 1879. The six mentioned above — the chief proponents of the movement — came from middle-class Protestant families; they attended eastern universities — Harvard, the University of Pennsylvania, and Bryn Mawr. They entered a world which had just rediscovered Troy, as the interest in Greek myth seen in Pound's *Cantos*, H. D.'s *Heliodora* and *Helen in Egypt*, Williams's *Kora in Hell*, and Moore's "An Octopus" still testifies. The retreat from industrialization and the concomitant reverence for the simple spirit of the Middle Ages expressed in John Ruskin's and William Morris's arts and crafts movement in Victorian England were not only still in the air when the modernists began to write; they were then making their first appearance in America, in Boston. Predicated on the notion that society produces the art and architecture it deserves, the philosophy of that movement affected the poets in many ways, from Pound's early Provençal lyrics to Williams's concern for his artist-contemporaries to Moore's insistent care for the art of the book. As men explored the last of the unknown continents and propelled themselves above the earth for the first time, the modernist poets undertook their own voyages: Pound into Greek, American, and Chinese history; Williams to "pagany" — the

sources of old Europe — only to rediscover his American roots and Paterson; Stevens with Crispin into the Floridian landscapes of the imagination; Eliot first to the decayed post-war society and later to Christian rebirth; Moore to the world of natural history where exotic flora and fauna bespoke moral values corroded by modern man.

The call of Europe beckoned to them all. Pound, H. D., and Eliot while in their twenties moved abroad. Williams studied at Leipzig and later took a sabbatical in France and Italy. Moore traveled to England when she could and an early trip to Britain and France left a deep imaginative presence. Stevens, though never leaving the States, became the compleat Francophile. The modernist movement which was to involve them all was, however, not confined to one continent. The three who did not move abroad became, in their different ways, leaders of the New York literary renaissance with close ties to the revolution Pound was encouraging from London, and later from Paris and Rapallo.

The verse these poets created reflected not only their informed interest in European culture; it also responded to the exploded surface of the West at the time of World War I, seeking in its shards and fragments the material for poetry. In a complete break with the poetry of the past, the new poetry contained quotations from and allusions to anything from renaissance politicians to *The New York Times*. It did not hesitate to embrace bits and pieces of archaeology, Chinese moral philosophy, Shakespeare, and the *National Geographic*. The splicing of such diverse material by what Pound called the "logic of juxtaposition" became its hallmark. The forms the poets developed to accommodate the fragments had irregular shapes and broken patterns sometimes called "free verse," but in fact, the forms were highly structured according to new rules which stressed "ordinary" speech. Marianne Moore's poetry became as modernist as that of her peers; at times her contemporaries found it even more revolutionary than their own.

Beginnings

Marianne Moore's place among her peers resulted not from early personal contact with her contemporaries nor from living in the cities where the revolution in poetry was taking place. In her years of development, she remained outside the charmed circles of Pound-Williams-H. D. in Philadelphia or Yeats-Pound-Eliot in London. Ultimately, she walked her own path to modernism, alone, in Carlisle, Pennsylvania; by the time she began to know her contemporaries, by mail at least, she had already formed herself as a poet.

Marianne's upbringing, however, set her amid the intellectual and cultural interests of her time. Born on November 15, 1887, at the manse of the First Presbyterian Church of Kirkwood, Missouri, a rather elegant suburb of St. Louis, she grew up in the home of her grandfather, the Reverend John R. Warner. Her mother had attended the Mary Institute in St. Louis, graduating from the superior class — somewhat equivalent to junior college today. Her father, an engineer with a degree from Stevens Institute, had had a nervous breakdown before Marianne's birth and been institutionalized; she never knew him.

At the manse, Marianne and her brother Warner, a little more than a year older, were surrounded by books to be both read and heard: Milton, Dickens, Sir Walter Scott and Jacob Abbott — particularly his Rollo books, filled with a young boy's travels in Europe — among them. The process of writing was apparent to them as their grandfather prepared his weekly sermon. After the Reverend Warner's death in 1894, the family moved to Pennsylvania to be near relatives, first to Allegheny City (now part of Pittsburgh) and then to Carlisle. The latter turned out to have a surprisingly literary atmosphere for the Moores.

After settling in Carlisle, Mrs. Moore was persuaded to teach English at the Metzger Institute, a Presbyterian school for girls across the street from her house. Marianne attended the school and for years the family took their meals there, dining with faculty and students (augmented at vacation time by three Benéts, Laura, William, and Stephen, grandchildren of a staff member).

Up the street lived the George Norcross family; they were to be a major influence on the course of Marianne's life. Dr. Norcross was pastor of the Second Presbyterian Church, the Moore's parish. His wife, Louise Jackson, was the sister of a well-known Presbyterian missionary to Alaska, Sheldon Jackson, whose introduction of reindeer into the Alaskan Indian economy was just the sort of event to inspire one of Marianne's poems years later. By 1900, three Norcross daughters had graduated from Bryn Mawr. The youngest, Mary, worked at the college for two years before returning to Carlisle to pursue a career in arts and crafts, enrolling for workshops at the Boston Society for Arts and Crafts founded by Charles Eliot Norton, professor of fine arts at Harvard. In 1904-05, Mary Norcross took on the task of preparing Marianne for Bryn Mawr, saw her through her matriculation examinations, and finally settled Marianne into her dormitory in October 1905. Mary later built near Carlisle a magnificent mountain home, all of chestnut and set among exotic flowers, according to plans in Gustav Stickley's *The Craftsman*. This close brush with the arts and crafts movement had something to do with Marianne's interest in the expertly-made object — the paper knife or the medieval decorated hatbox — which she worked into her poems.

When Marianne entered the class of 1909 at Bryn Mawr, she stepped into a new world. At its core were classes in English — lectures, composition, and elocution — Latin, biology, philosophy, Italian, psychology, and later a major in history-politics-economics. An English major was denied her, with one professor remarking: "Please a little lucidity! Your obscurity becomes greater and greater;" and another: "You have narrative and descriptive ability I think but you must pay more attention to the requirements." One course stood out: "Imitative Writing," taught by Georgiana Goddard King, concentrated on the well-known seventeenth-century stylists Bacon, Browne, Andrewes, Traherne, Hooker, and Burton. Taken in her last semester, this course offered a sharp contrast to Marianne's college-years writing style as seen in the eight short stories and eight poems published in the undergraduate magazine, *Tipyn o'Bob*. The principles of style emphasized by Miss King made a deep impression, however, and Marianne drew upon them as she developed her mature style.

As an editor of *Tipyn o'Bob*, Marianne found herself in a bit of a literary whirl; even the college president, M. Carey Thomas, remarked in chapel on her work, casting favor upon the poems and disfavor upon the stories. Friends with a literary bent — Peggy James, William's daughter and Henry's niece, Margaret Ayer, later a Pulitzer Prize-winning novelist, and Marcet Haldeman, future publisher of the "Little Blue Book" series of condensed classics — made for lively conversations about extracurricular reading in Meredith, Stevenson, Scott, Kipling, Tennyson, and Henry James.

Marianne's letters home reveal that the desire to write invaded her during her sophomore year, causing a conflict with duties assigned in classes. Her poems and stories foreshadow her later writing. Although she declared in her letters that she labored over the prose and dashed off the verse, the drafts she sent home for inspection were all poems. A poem she called "Ennui" attracted the attention of a Greek professor who made much of it in class (in which Marianne was not a student) because he was intrigued by its meter, pronounced by him to be "dithrambic glyconic." The poem reads:

He often expressed a curious wish
to be interchangeably man and fish
to nibble the bait off the hook, said he
and then slip away like a ghost in the sea.

Marianne delighted in Dr. Saunders's interest,

which extended even to his revision of the poem in order to perfect the meter, a change Marianne did not employ, any more than she would accept Pound's rearrangement of the ending of "A Grave" a decade later. Her notions of meter were already forming in non-accentual patterns. Inspiration for "Ennui" came with the appearance of the Ben Greet players who performed *The Tempest* at the college. Marianne was taken by Greet's portrayal of Caliban who, she said, appeared to be half man, half fish. Twenty-five years later, Marianne borrowed the first two lines of "Ennui" for "The Pangolin."

Another college poem, "A Jelly-Fish," began in the biology laboratory and was continued during Imitative Writing class. A surviving laboratory notebook contains detailed drawings of the jellyfish, a creature Marianne had surely seen on vacations at Cape May, New Jersey, or on Monhegan Island, Maine. The first few lines of the poem are entered in her class notes and appear in a letter home, followed by a poem addressed to Longinus, whose essay on aesthetics, "On the Sublime," had been assigned by Miss King. After publication in Bryn Mawr's alumnae magazine, *The Lantern*, "A Jelly-Fish" lay dormant until Marianne resurrected it for *The Trinity Review* in 1957.

These early efforts foreshadow what were to be life-long habits: a choice of subject matter close at hand and conservation of poetic material for later use.

The eight short stories Marianne wrote for *Tipyn o'Bob* were her only efforts in that genre until a single attempt in the 1930s. Each story turns on the moment of a youth's shift from childhood to maturity. All but two protagonists are painters or writers who struggle to pursue a questioned talent. A medieval setting governs four stories, a contemporary one the others.

The medieval settings for her stories arose easily from the English curriculum required for freshmen. Far more dramatic an instance of the prevalent medieval fever, however, was the May Day festival held in the spring of her freshman year, a quadrennial event which seemed to grow right out of the college's Oxbridgian towers, porticos, and gargoyles. Marianne reports having "had the middle ages badly at seventeen," and May Day must have escalated that tendency. Every student took a costumed role, from the king and queen of the May to Morris dancers and the great worthies (including Julius Caesar, David, and Judas Maccabeus). Medieval masques were performed at four stations on the lawns, and white oxen pulled enormous maypoles in the grand procession. Marianne, garbed in green brocade, served as an attendant to the royal court. The preparations required after-class rehearsals for the entire semester. Hilda Doolittle, Marianne's classmate, but a day student and barely known by her, invited William Carlos Williams to the celebration but did not introduce him to his future fellow-poet.

Georgiana Goddard King's class is probably the setting for the most significant literary development at college for Marianne. While T. S. Eliot is credited with rediscovering the seventeenth century for the modernist generation, his "Metaphysical Poets" did not appear until 1921 when he reviewed Grierson's anthology for the *Times Literary Supplement.* His essays on seventeenth-century prose writers were published still later. Moore's study of seventeenth-century prose in 1909 took her to the writers those poets themselves were reading, from Bacon's humanistic essays to the sermons of Protestant divines. The rhythms of the King James Bible, the devices of classical rhetoric, and the careful splicing of eclectic subject matter characteristic of that prose were to influence not only her prose, but also the *materia poetica* she was to choose for her verse, so evident in the famous bibliographical notes she appended to her poems.

Miss King seems to have been Marianne's link to contemporary writers as well. In a notebook she kept at the time, Marianne wrote: "Ezra Pound — — at all costs!" King knew Gertrude Stein and Alfred Stieglitz, already "making it new" in Paris and New York, and might well have reported on the December 1908 review of Pound's *A Lume Spento* in the New York *Ameri-*

can Journal Examiner. In that review, Ella Wheeler Wilcox quoted extensively from the book and identified Pound as a Philadelphia poet who lived abroad. Marianne might have seen any of the seven articles Pound had published by that time in *Book News Monthly,* a Philadelphia periodical, although his translations of late medieval Latin verse were his only poetry to appear there. The enthusiasm of her notebook entry suggests a strong recommendation, in any case, and one Marianne was to act on soon.

The summer of 1911 found Marianne and her mother in England and France. This momentous trip is recorded in not nearly enough detail in letters to her brother, but the itinerary and some of its highlights survive, as does Marianne's marked Baedeker. The Moores sailed from Philadelphia to Liverpool and began a tour which took them north to the Lake District, Sterling, Glasgow, Edinburgh, and back into England through York, Lincoln, Stratford, and Oxford to London. Art galleries, historic monuments, and literary shrines filled the summer. Sterling Castle and Robert Burns's country appealed to their Scotch-Irish ancestry, as did Carlyle's house in London. Collections of armor reinforced an early interest: "I shan't be satisfied now till we have an armoury," Marianne told her brother. A long, hot pilgrimage to William Morris's Kelmscott was scantly rewarded by a view only of its garden, but Marianne remarks on seeing work by Morris, Burne-Jones, and the other pre-Raphaelites in Glasgow and London. The British Museum, Westminster Abbey, Hampton Court, the new museum in Kensington (now the Victoria and Albert), the National Portrait Gallery, and the other Baedeker essentials all received visits. July thirteenth in London brought together two of Marianne's particular enthusiasms: the London Zoo and Elkin Mathews's book shop where she purchased the books by Ezra Pound then in print, *Personae* and *Exultations.*

On the eighth of August the travelers crossed to Paris where they stayed on the Left Bank. The Louvre's "rotten Rubens" displeased Marianne, but she expressed excitement at its Assyrian gallery and its Dürers. The Odeon book shop, "the literary oracle of Paris," and Victor Hugo's house, "the most spine-quaking museum," left their lasting and usable impressions. Purchases included a photograph of Rodin's *Penseur* and a copy of Dumas's *Le Chevalier de Maison Rouge*. When the Moores returned to Philadelphia from Le Havre, they had been away exactly three months.

It would be hard to overestimate the importance of this trip to Marianne's writing. While much of what she saw went unrecorded, descriptions in her letters turn up years later in poems: peacocks amid cedar trees and the armory at Warwick Castle appear in "People's Surroundings," a swan at Oxford becomes the swan in "Critics and Connoisseurs," Elizabethan sweetmeat trenchers at the Bodleian Library inspire "Counseil to a Bacheler," the ceiling and the stalls in St. George's Chapel at Windsor seem to be those of "The Pangolin," the "revolving diamond rosette" at Whitehall occurs in "Tell Me, Tell Me," Victor Hugo is the springboard for "To Victor Hugo of My Crow Pluto," and a terrier in Salisbury makes an appearance in "Picking and Choosing." Although these images are but details in a larger picture, they underscore a lasting contribution to Marianne's store of experiences later to be mined for poetic material.

This trip abroad was an important episode during a period resembling a rather hidden life for Marianne, the years between college and her first appearance in a little magazine. The evidence drawn from her college years makes clear that she wanted writing as a career. In her last semester at Bryn Mawr, she had submitted a poem to *The Atlantic* and received her first rejection slip. She had also interviewed, without success, for work at the *Ladies' Home Journal* in Philadelphia. Told by her interviewer to acquire secretarial skills if she wanted a career in publishing, she followed this advice and enrolled in the Carlisle Commercial College that summer; she graduated a year later.

Her first job, one she never mentioned in print, took her to the Lake Placid Club in upstate New York where Melvil Dewey administered both his resort and his famous Decimal System for libraries. Marianne's duties included typing Dewey's letters in the reformed spelling he promoted (and which accounted for the missing "le" at the end of his first name) and filing. After two months, she was let go, either in order to reduce the staff for the winter or by mutual agreement; she admitted to her mother that she felt unsuited to the kind of detailed, high-pressured work given her. Nearly a year separated the end of the Lake Placid job and her next as teacher of business subjects at the United States Indian School in Carlisle where she was to stay until the summer of 1914.

Although her work at the Indian School consumed her days and many evenings, Marianne found time to read and to work at poems. She began to submit work to both popular and little magazines, even daring to send a pseudonymous entry to William Rose Benét, then at *The Century*. She gathered sixty poems for submission to a contest for a book of poetry, but her work was not chosen. She kept a commonplace book which reveals an extraordinary breadth of reading. Among the publications available to her were *The Literary Digest* which excerpted articles from British and American literary, scientific, political, and religious magazines; *The Outlook*, a Christian journal edited by Henry Ward Beecher and Lyman Abbott; *The Illustrated London News* with its columns on archaeology, antiques, and natural history; *The National Geographic*; *The Boston Evening Transcript* whose book and drama reviews she admired; *The English Review* edited by Ford Madox Ford; *The Spectator* (London); and *Scribner's Magazine*.

A new library had opened in Carlisle in 1909 and the larger library in Harrisburg lay a short train-ride away. Occasionally, Marianne went to Washington to read at the Library of Congress and to visit the Smithsonian Institution. She kept a series of small commonplace books filled with reading notes — chiefly from prose. A list of readings from one brief period includes Poe's *Philosophy of Composition*; *The Literati of New York* by FitzGreene Halleck; William Lyons Phelps in the *Yale Review; Diversions in Sicily* by H. F. Jones; Hegel's *Philosophy of History;* an article on John Dewey's philosophy of education; *Modern Painting* by W. W. Wright; and Synge's *The Aran Islands,* to name only a few. Such intense preparation, writing fed by reading, for what must have seemed at the time a will-'o-the wisp career, finally yielded two acceptances from little magazines.

An Emerging Modernist

In 1912, Harriet Monroe had launched *Poetry: A Magazine of Verse* in Chicago, and in 1913, Harriet Shaw Weaver had taken the helm of *The Egoist* in London. Pound proclaimed imagism in *Poetry* in that year, the same year that modern art — Brancusi's *Kiss* and Duchamp's *Nude Descending a Staircase* — jolted New Yorkers at the Armory Show. Pound and Wyndham Lewis crystalized wartime turbulence by announcing vorticism through their 1914-1915 magazine, *Blast,* whose visual jerkiness was not unlike that of Charlie Chaplin's *Little Angel* or *The Perils of Pauline* then playing in the movie houses. Despite the war in Europe, and partly in response to it, a literary renaissance had emerged by 1915. It was to change forever the history of poetry in English.

1915 marks the year of Moore's first professional publications. The midpoint of a remarkable decade for arts and letters, it was the year of Virginia Woolf's *The Voyage Out,* Ezra Pound's *Cathay,* and Kafka's *Metamorphosis.* D. H. Lawrence's *The Rainbow* appeared in September and was banned in November; Robert Frost's *North of Boston* had to seek a publisher far north of Boston, in fact in England. The talented young sculptor Henri Gaudier-Brzeska died in the war and John Quinn, the New York patron of artists and writers, bought Gaudier's magnificent stone cat as well as paintings by Wyndham Lewis. The United States had not yet entered the war in Europe, and Henry James offended Americans by renouncing his citizenship.

From submissions sent in 1914, Harriet Weaver at *The Egoist* and Harriet Monroe at *Poetry* each took a group of poems to be published respectively in April and May 1915. Of all the magazines to which Moore sent poems, no others could have brought her work to the attention of the day's poet-lions as well as those two. Ezra Pound had close ties to both magazines; Richard Aldington, and by 1916, his wife, Hilda Doolittle, worked for *The Egoist,* as did T. S. Eliot a little later; *Poetry,* as of its 32nd issue in May 1915, had published all the major modernist poets except Eliot, whose first professional publication would occur in the next issue with "The Love Song of J. Alfred Prufrock." Thus did Moore join the best possible company of poets.

An examination of the May 1915 issue of *Poetry* reveals the company with whom Moore first appeared. It also points to the literary publications which came to her attention through her reading of little magazines. The issue contained poetry by Joseph Warren Beach, a Harvard Ph.D. and later an influential critic of twentieth-century verse; Floyd Dell, radical editor of *The Masses;* Maurice Browne, whose Chicago Little Theater had already contributed forcefully to the artistic renaissance in that city; William Carlos Williams, whom Monroe calls "a prominent member of the imagist group"; and six other poets who cannot be said ever to have embraced the modernist spirit. Prose included the third installment of Pound's essay, "The Renaissance," which called for subsidies for artists; reviews of books by James Stevens and Witter Bynner; a letter to the editor from Edgar Lee Masters who reports hearing that New York is becoming nearly as lively as Chicago and that should there be a

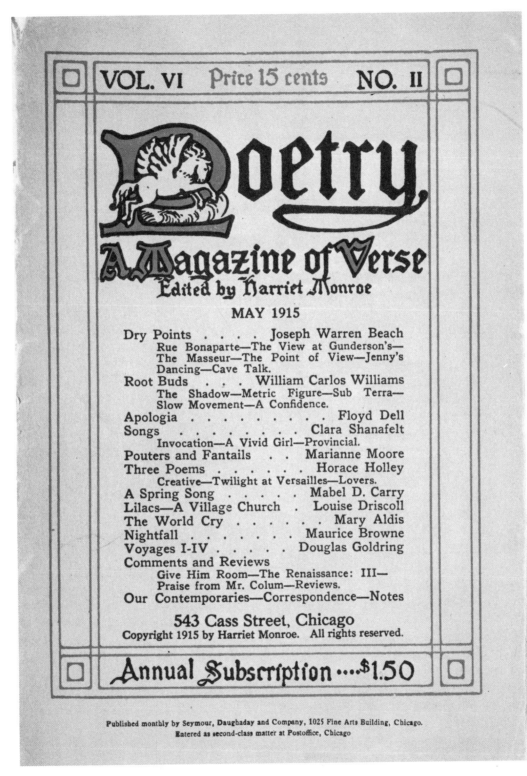

VOL. VI Price 15 cents NO. II

Poetry

A Magazine of Verse

Edited by Harriet Monroe

MAY 1915

543 Cass Street, Chicago
Copyright 1915 by Harriet Monroe. All rights reserved.

Annual Subscription $1.50

Published monthly by Seymour, Daughaday and Company, 1025 Fine Arts Building, Chicago.
Entered as second-class matter at Postoffice, Chicago

Poetry, May 1915

"renascence" in American poetry, it could be traced to *Poetry* (a forecast in which he was entirely correct); and Alice Corbin Henderson's blast at Amy Lowell for her foolish misunderstanding of Frost's *North of Boston* as "photographic" realism "unchanged by any personal mental process." In addition, *Some Imagist Poets: An Anthology*, which Amy Lowell had virtually wrested away from Pound, is advertised on the back cover. Another advertisement lists the six books of poems by Pound then in print; another announces a special imagist number of *The Egoist* including Pound, Aldington, H. D., D. H. Lawrence, May Sinclair, Amy Lowell, and Marianne Moore.

One can only imagine Moore's surprise at the *Egoist* advertisement. It led at once to a warning from William Benét not to get herself mixed up with *that* school and to her often repeated disavowal of membership in it. But inclusion, however protested, in such a revolutionary group gave Moore's work extraordinary visibility among her peers from the moment of her first publication.

Of the five poems which appeared in *Poetry* and the two in the April *Egoist*, only "To Military Progress," a strongly worded anti-war statement, survived among her collected work. All seven poems reflect a serious moral stance fundamental to Moore's biblically-informed world view. The clearest example is "Appellate Jurisdiction" in which she comments on St. Paul's discussion of sin and redemption in his epistle to the Romans. "That Harp You Play So Well" contrasts David the psalmist with the King David who sent his armies against his son, Absalom. "The Wizard in Words," later called "Reticence and Volubility," is a dialogue between the pagan and the believer, cast as Merlin's recognition that Dante's allegory stood for truth. Moore's later poetry, while less explicitly religious in expression, continues to explore the ideas announced in this early work: humility, forgiveness, faith, and tolerance.

The other short pieces suggest directions which Moore's poetry would take. "To an Intramural Rat" is a critique of an unnamed poet who "once met [would] be forgot again;/Or merely resurrected/In a parenthesis of wit." (Rat, from the character in *The Wind in the Willows*, was Moore family parlance for poet.) "Counseil to a Bacheler" places a footnote in the position of an epigraph: "Elizabethan Trencher Motto — Bodleian Library: [with title and modification of second line]." In fact, the four-line poem is an adjusted quotation with credit given but without quotation marks, a practice which later characterized nearly every poem. Finally, in "To a Man Working His Way through the Crowd," Moore assigns Gordon Craig, the revolutionary set designer, the characteristics of a lynx — here high praise — a device which would become prominent in her work.

Ten more poems followed in 1915 in *The Egoist*, and in December, in Alfred Kreymborg's new magazine, *Others*, an enterprise supported by William Carlos Williams. During the year she continued to send out poems and received rejections from *The Yale Review*, *T. P.'s Weekly*, and *Poetry*. By July, Moore knew her work was beginning to attract attention. Richard Aldington mentioned her in *Greenwich Village*, however briefly. On September eighth, Hilda Doolittle wrote to Moore in care of Bryn Mawr College to ask whether the poet whose work appeared in *The Egoist* were the same Marianne Moore whom she knew at school. After praising Moore's "technical ability," she suggested that Moore come to London to live — a theme she renewed several times over the next decade. For Moore, however, there was literary excitement much closer to home.

Moore made a one-week trip to New York that presaged the stimulus that city would later have for her as its resident. In late November, she stayed with friends at the YWCA National Training School at 135 East 52nd Street where she attended classes in public speaking and on the Book of Isaiah. Off on her own, she dined with Alfred and Gertrude Kreymborg. At their apartment she was shown photographs by Alfred Stieglitz and Edward Steichen and spoke with her hosts about the poetry of Amy Lowell, Ezra Pound, and Richard Aldington. With Laura Benét she visited Laura's brother William, then on the editorial staff at *The Century*. At the Daniel Gallery she saw paintings and embroideries by William and Marguerite Zorach (Marguerite would paint Moore's portrait ten years later). A "magnificent" photograph of Whitman attracted her attention at the Kraft Gallery. At 291 Fifth Avenue, she met Alfred Stieglitz, the redoubtable photographer and promoter of modern art. Stieglitz showed her paintings by Picasso, Picabia, and Marsden Hartley, and gave her copies of his *Camera Work*, particularly one containing his photograph of Gordon Craig which she much admired. He introduced her to J. B. Kerfoot, a drama critic for *Life* whose work she had often seen, and they discussed his recent review of a Shaw play. One afternoon, she climbed to Guido Bruno's garret office on Washington Square, the home of *Bruno's Weekly*, *Bruno's Chap Books*, and other avant-garde, if short-lived, publications. Bruno had just brought out a chap book containing Richard Aldington's essay, "The Imagists," which stated that Moore "shows promise." He was to publish Moore's poems in his *Weekly* the following year. This remarkable week in 1915, detailed in a series of lengthy letters to her brother over the course of the next month, while not her first trip to New York, clearly left its mark. Three years later, faced with having to move, Moore went unhesitatingly to Greenwich Village.

By the end of 1915, Marianne Moore had published seventeen poems, had come to the attention of the writers who were to be most important to her, and had affirmed her intention to become a writer. She had stopped teaching at the Indian School in the summer of 1914 and had begun to look for literary work. Attempts to become a reviewer for the *Philadelphia Ledger* and other papers came to nothing. The Moores knew that before too long Marianne's brother, Warner, who had finished his degree in divinity at the Princeton Theological Seminary, would be appointed a pastor, and when that happened, Moore and her mother would move with him to

his manse. Indeed, that change came about in September, 1916. The family moved to the Ogdon Memorial Presbyterian Church in Chatham, New Jersey. Exactly two years later, after Warner had joined the Navy Chaplain's Corps and given up his parish, they moved again, now to 14 St. Luke's Place, in Greenwich Village.

While Marianne Moore continued to publish poems, she began to submit prose as well. A long article on the tone of voice in poetry came out in *The Egoist* in 1916 and three reviews appeared in *Poetry* in 1918. The reviews concerned poetry by contemporaries: Jean de Bosschère's poems translated by F. S. Flint, T. S. Eliot's *Prufrock and Other Observations*, and W. B. Yeats's *Wild Swans at Coole*. *The New York Times* asked her to review Robert Lynd's *Old and New Masters in Literature;* Moore takes on Lynd's views of James and Hardy in language that recurred the next year in her poem, "Picking and Choosing." While in Chatham, she received her first visit from William Carlos Williams and his wife, and after her move to New York, she began to correspond with Ezra Pound. In just a few years, Moore had become a full-scale member of the modernist circle.

In these years, Marianne Moore's poetry reached a maturity that contrasts sharply with the accomplishments that brought her into that circle in 1915. "Critics and Connoisseurs," in the issue of *Others* edited by Williams in 1916, portrays a hungry swan and a busy ant pursuing "ambition without understanding." The poem is one of the first to make use of the long lines, invisible rhyme, and elaborate syllabic meter which became Moore's hallmark. The opening sentence, "There is a great amount of poetry in unconscious /fastidiousness," and its example, "a/mere childish attempt to make an imperfectly ballasted/animal stand up," combines two important elements. In the first, latinate clause, the poet exhibits the kind of philosophic language Eliot thought to be an American phenomenon, the result of "universal university education." In the example of the pet, she begins to extend her definition of her own *materia poetica* to include her

11

observations of the natural world.

"Poetry," by far Moore's most famous poem (adumbrated in 1967 to its first three lines, with the whole poem as a footnote), appeared in *Others* in July 1919. Here she argues that poetry can embrace any subject as long as it is made by "literalists of the imagination" (from Yeats) out of "the raw material of poetry in/all its rawness and /that which is...genuine." Then, she says, we shall have "imaginary gardens with real toads in them." By this time, the rhythms of speech and of conversation clearly dominate her work. An unpublished poem of the same period called "Why That Question" wonders aloud "What is the difference between prose and poetry — /If it is one?" and answers, "there may/Be a difference, only no one says so who is sure...." Concern for a natural rhythm would cause Moore to rework some highly structured poems into seemingly free verse a few years later.

While these poems in no way suggest an affinity with the imagist poems of H. D. or Pound's imagist exemplum, "In a Station of the Metro," they do follow the dictates Pound set forth in 1913 — in their own way. His "direct treatment," no extra words, and musical phrase can be seen, characteristically reinterpreted by her, in a poem like "Picking and Choosing." A critique of arts and letters, this poem begins with a discussion of aesthetics:

> Literature is a phase of life. If one is afraid
> of it,
> the situation is irremediable; if one approaches
> it familiarly,
> what one says of it is worthless.
> • • •
> Why cloud the fact
> that Shaw is self-conscious in the field of
> sentiment
> but is otherwise rewarding; that James
> is all that has been said of him.

It closes with an image which combines an obser-

vation made in London in 1911 and a remark in Xenophon's *Cyngeticus:*

> Small dog, going over the lawn nipping the
> linen and saying
> that you have a badger — remember
> Xenophon;
> only rudimentary behavior is necessary to put
> us on the scent.
> "A right good salvo of barks," a few strong
> wrinkles puckering
> the skin between the ears, is all we ask.

That poem appeared in 1916. In 1917, Pound wrote in "Homage to Sextus Propertius:"

> And you write of Achelous, who contended
> with Hercules,
> You write of Adrastus' horses and the funeral
> rites of Achenor,
> And you will not leave off imitating Aeschylus.
> Though you make a hash of Antimachus,
> You think you are going to do Homer.
> • • •
> Like a trained and performing tortoise,
> I would make verse in your fashion...
> One must have resonance, resonance and
> sonority
> ...like a goose.

Pound's lines, while far less inverted or filled with archaisms than some he was writing just before this poem, contain slang — always part of his informal vocabulary — which rubs against his ancient subject. Moore's, on the other hand, have her own speech — including words like "irremediable," "rewarding," "rudimentary." Pound attempts "direct treatment" of a tortoise and a goose; Moore is far more specific, outlining a particular dog to exposit her satire. Neither poet indulges in wordiness. But two poems concerning a similar subject, written about the same time, illustrate differences of practice while striving toward a similar ideal.

Remy de Gourmont, writing on the imagists in 1915, makes the goals of the new poetry even clearer than Pound's dicta:

Les imagistes anglais procedent évidement des symbolistes français. On voit cela tout d'abord à leur horreur du cliché, l'horreur de la rhétorique et du grandiose, du genre oratoire, genre facile dont les imitateurs de Victor Hugo (anglicé, Swinburne, Tennyson, and Thompson) nous ont degoutés à jamais. Comme préceptes positifs, ils veulent la précision du language, la netteté de la vision, la concentration de la pensée qu'ils aiment à synthetiser dans une image dominante.*

While Marianne Moore certainly was not influenced by the French symbolists (Pound told her that he thought Jules Laforgue was a model, but she had never read him), other points de Gourmont makes do apply. She certainly shared the horror of clichés and of grandiloquent speech; and she strove always for precise language, sharp vision, and concentrated thought behind an image. That she succeeded was made clear by her lack of popularity, in the sense that Edna St. Vincent Millay was popular, and by the contrasting admiration of the leaders of modernism. In later years, she would echo the opening of Pound's "Salvationists" (1914): "Come, my songs, let us speak of perfection — /We shall get ourselves rather disliked." Frequently she rephrased the second line: "We shall get ourselves very much disliked."

The distance between the modernists and other poets during these years could be measured in large part by likes and dislikes. In 1918, a curious rupture took place, separating the modernists from their early patroness, Harriet Monroe at *Poetry*. Writing in the *English Review* in May,

Edgar Jepson characterized *Poetry* as a magazine so American that it would turn American art away from Europe and towards the western interests of Vachel Lindsay and Edgar Lee Masters. Indeed, from the beginning of the magazine, Pound had complained to Monroe that she was too taken with simplistic autochthonous poets. True, Monroe did publish poems in praise of hog-butchers alongside those of the imagists and Eliot. The effect of Jepson's article, and of replies by Monroe and several newspaper critics, was to alienate the very writers who had been most helped by *Poetry* and who were, we now know, the most enduringly illustrious guests at the feast Monroe had provided.

Monroe had rejected everything Moore sent her after the group of poems published in May 1915. In May 1918, probably having read the Jepson article or at least aware of its import, Moore in effect parted ways with Monroe. In her last letter to the magazine until 1931, she wrote: "Poetry's approach to art is different from my own; I feel it therefore to be very good of you to imply that I am not ipso facto an alien." Pound, Williams, Eliot, Stevens, and H. D. also disappeared from *Poetry's* pages until after 1930.

One magazine to which the modernists moved during the interim was *The Dial*. For Marianne Moore, it became more than a literary home; as editor from 1925 to 1929, it was to be in large part her creation.

* The imagists writing in English owe their beginnings to the French symbolists. We see this primarily in their loathing for the cliché, for rhetoric and pretentiousness, for oratory, that glib style used by Victor Hugo's imitators (in English, Swinburne, Tennyson, and Thompson) who have always repelled us. According to their constant rule, they seek precision of language, sharpness of vision, and compressed thought from which they like to draw a prevailing image.

The Dial

Ezra Pound said, in *Poetry* in 1913, that he had made a pact with Walt Whitman. "I have detested you long enough," he announced in his poem, "A Pact"; "We have one sap and one root — /Let there be commerce between us." But by 1919 he was to say to Marianne Moore that the

Whitman slogan always printed on the back cover of *Poetry* stood for the enemy: "To have great poets/there must be great audiences too," the magazine claimed in gothic type. Harriet Monroe, Pound thought, had had a failure of nerve and allowed too much inferior writing to appear in the magazine, perhaps to pander to a wider public than could be reached by difficult modernist verse.

The little magazines which had spread the renaissance were changing or disappearing. *Poetry* seemed to have retreated from the front ranks, and most of the Chicago members of the renaissance had moved to New York. *The Egoist* was about to fail, *The Little Review* would soon be suppressed for publishing *Ulysses*, and *Others* had run its course. A few brave efforts at new little magazines tried to carry on the excitement — Williams's and Robert McAlmon's *Contact* and Matthew Josephson's *Broom* — but the coming Jazz Age called for something else.

Two young, wealthy, literary Harvard graduates stepped in. In 1919, Scofield Thayer and James Sibley Watson Jr. purchased a magazine that thought of itself as the continuation of Margaret Fuller's and Emerson's *Dial*. Reborn as a Chicago journal in 1880, *The Dial* moved to New York in 1918 and became, in the hands of the brilliant Randolph Bourne, a respected magazine of literary and social commentary. Bourne died soon after this move.

Thayer had contributed to the support of Bourne's *Dial*, a magazine of considerable prominence. When after Bourne's death the magazine foundered, he and Watson bought it with the intent of shaping it into their own modernist journal. From the beginning, they made careful plans for their periodical to be devoted exclusively to arts and letters, from its design by the noted typographer Bruce Rogers to the departments to be covered each month. They attracted Thomas Mann to write about German literary affairs, Pound to write from Paris, Eliot from London, and John Eglinton from Dublin. Thayer, who had begun to collect paintings and drawings in Europe, festooned each issue with a four-color frontispiece and several black-and-white plates.

In the first volume, which began in January 1920, Cézanne, Charles Demuth, John Marin, Gaston Lachaise, and Charles Burchfield were among the artists represented. Writers whose prose appeared during the first six months included such diverse luminaries as Bertrand Russell and Conrad Aiken. Others whose work appeared in the first volume are: John Dewey, Henry McBride (later the resident art critic), Kenneth Burke, James Stevens, Malcolm Cowley, Sherwood Anderson, Bertrand Russell, Babette Deutsch, E. E. Cummings, Edmund Wilson, John Dos Passos, Van Wyck Brooks, and William Butler Yeats.

Among the poets in the first volume, those we remember best today are Conrad Aiken, Robert Hillyer, Maxwell Bodenheim, Carl Sandburg, Witter Bynner, Alfred Kreymborg, E. E. Cummings, Ezra Pound, Amy Lowell, Edna St. Vincent Millay, Louis Untermeyer, A. E., Hart Crane, Djuna Barnes, and Marianne Moore.

Of the hundreds of books reviewed, those by these authors were commented upon in the first volume: Conrad Aiken, Donn Byrne, Gilbert Cannan, Chekhov, Chesterton, Samuel Clemens, Gordon Craig, Gabriele D'Annunzio, Dostoyevski, E. M. Forster, Paul Gauguin, Thomas Hardy, Dean Inge, William Dean Howells, Aldous Huxley, Henry James, James Joyce, John Maynard Keynes, Amy Lowell, Maurice Maeterlinck, Edgar Lee Masters, H. L. Mencken, Lytton Strachey, Turgenev, and Sidney and Beatrice Webb.

Co-owner Watson wrote on Rimbaud under the name of W. C. Blum; Thayer published some verse under his own name. The poets printed in the first volume show nearly as catholic an aesthetic as that of Harriet Monroe, with Carl Sandburg and Pound representing the extremes. Nearly 300 book reviews, either long essays or one-paragraph "Briefer Mentions," discussed work by writers of every stripe and genre. This volume, comprising only the first six issues, demonstrates the scope sought for the magazine by its young originators. If F. Scott Fitzgerald, William Faulkner, and Ernest Hemingway never appeared in *The Dial*, among writers in Europe and in the United States who became prominent in the 1920s they were exceptions.

Two anecdotes tell of Moore's entrance into *The Dial's* circle. In the first, she had been asked to read at a literary gathering and she chose her poem "England." Thayer listened and asked her to send the poem to his magazine. Moore said she had, but without success. It appeared in the April 1920 issue. In the second, Ezra Pound is seen taking on his customary role as advisor to editors. Although he had read very little of Moore's writing other than her poetry, he counseled Thayer to ask her for prose. Thayer did, and Moore produced more than a hundred "Briefer Mentions," thirty essays, and forty editor's "Comments," a prodigious body of work over nine years.

When she arrived in New York in the fall of 1918, Marianne Moore was the only modernist poet in the city. She and her mother moved into a tiny apartment at 14 St. Luke's Place, a handsome block east of Seventh Avenue just above Houston Street. New York's literary renaissance grew as Chicago's faded. *The Little Review* moved from the Windy City to Manhattan in 1917; *Others*, led by Kreymborg and Williams, was in full swing. The far left was represented by *The Masses*, edited by Max Eastman, Floyd Dell, and John Reed, who along with socialists Emma Goldman and Lincoln Steffens frequented Mabel Dodge's salon on Fifth Avenue. And across Washington Square, the Provincetown Players had two years earlier opened their first New York season on MacDougal Street. Lola Ridge, who had worked on Kreymborg's *Others* and later on *Broom*, was a dedicated party-giver; to her apartment came the poets and painters who welcomed Moore into their midst.

Soon after her move to St. Luke's Place, Moore applied for work at the Hudson Park Branch of the New York Public Library. Just across the street from her apartment, the library proved to

be an excellent part-time job, and in the fall of 1920 she passed the librarian's examination in current events, literature, and French.

By then, she had begun to publish in *The Dial* and had come to know Thayer and Watson. In September, she was invited to *The Dial's* office at 153 West 13th Street to have tea and to meet the staff. She brought along her review of the poems of Jacopone da Todi, the medieval mystic whose work had been resurrected by Evelyn Underhill. Thayer not only accepted the review but also offered Moore her selection of books to be critiqued in "Briefer Mentions." A few weeks later, Thayer asked her to tea at his apartment on Washington Square where he showed her his collection of modern art.

Outside *The Dial's* offices, other supporters campaigned for Moore's work. Richard Aldington wrote to Harriet Monroe in August, naming Moore as his first choice to receive a prize from *Poetry*, despite her not having published poems there since 1915. He sent Monroe another note in December to reaffirm his confidence in Moore's poetry. Pound had mentioned her in an article in *Future* in 1918 and reprinted the piece in *Instigations*, published in New York in April 1920. The next spring, T. S. Eliot wrote to say that he had admired her work since he first saw it in *Others* in 1917 and to suggest that he might help her publish a book of poems. Amy Lowell invited Moore to hear her lecture at Columbia; her letter suggests that they had had previous correspondence. Yvor Winters told her that she should try to publish a book. William Carlos Williams, by now an acquaintance, introduced two of her poems in an essay in his new magazine *Contact*, which he edited with Robert McAlmon. Hilda Doolittle continued in her supportive role, both in her letters to Moore and in the pages of *The Egoist*. However, for all this attention, Moore still had not published a volume of her poems nor planned one. Hilda Doolittle and McAlmon would take this matter into their own hands within a year.

Late in 1920, H. D. — as Hilda Doolittle had become known — and Winifred Ellerman — who had changed her name to Bryher — passed through New York on their way to Carmel, California, where Moore had lined up a cottage for their stay. When they returned to New York in February, Moore hosted a tea for them so that they could meet Thayer and Watson. The tea turned into a wedding reception since, unknown to the others, Bryher and McAlmon had been married at City Hall that afternoon. During their visit Bryher and H. D. put pressure on Moore to allow them to publish a collection of her poems. Moore held back but to no avail. On July 10, 1921, she received copies of *Poems* by Marianne Moore, published by Harriet Shaw Weaver at the Egoist Press, paid for by Bryher. H. D., Bryher, and McAlmon had taken two dozen poems published in *The Dial*, *The Egoist*, *Others*, and *Contact*, and had them printed in a 24-page booklet with heavy paper covers, wrapped in pottery-colored patterned paper. Moore's response was guarded gratitude.

Harriet Monroe decided to test the book in her magazine with a "Symposium," a vigorous, partly acrimonious debate of its merits. Written by herself, with quotations from others, Monroe's review marshalls opprobrium toward a condemnation that sounds like sour grapes, perhaps in reaction to *Poetry's* having lost to other magazines the most highly regarded poets it had yet published. She acknowledges her stance at the beginning: "Miss Moore's steely and recondite art has long been a rallying-point for the radicals." She questions whether the author of "the geometrical verse-designs which frame these cryptic observations" is a poet. Then, in the manner of a debator, she lets the opposition speak. First, H. D., who says Marianne Moore "is a poet;" then Yvor Winters:

With the exception of Wallace Stevens, she is about the only poet since Rimbaud who has had any very profound or intricate command of sound; and I am not sure but I think her about the best poet in this country except for Mr. Stevens.

Bryher is allowed the next "pro" statement, a plea meant to entice Moore to Europe:

Her *Poems* are an important addition to American literature, to the entire literature of the modern world. Only, Marco Polo, your sword is ready and your kingdoms wait. May it soon please you to leave the fireside and ride forth.

Speaking for the opposition is Marion Strobel, an associate editor at *Poetry*:

...because we are conscious that she has brains, that she is exceedingly well-informed, we are the more irritated that she has not learned to write simply.

And "another poet-critic, Pearl Andelson" says:

Marianne Moore has much the Emily Dickinson type of mind, but where Emily Dickinson's not infrequent obscurities arise out of an authentic mysticism, Marianne Moore's are more likely the result of a relentless discipline in the subtler "ologies" and "osophies." ...[some of her poems] are hybrids of a flagrantly prose origin.

Monroe then carries on, citing "the grim and haughty humor of this lady" and, while admiring her wit, proposes that "a deep resistless humor like Miss Moore's" may become "the most subtly corrosive destroyer of genius." Monroe's less formal dismissal can be discerned from her annotation on the original letter from Yvor Winters quoted in part in the review. Monroe left out his phrase "a very great poet," and in the margin of the letter, wrote "Piffle."

Strong reactions marked all responses to Moore's book, not least her own. Upon hearing from her brother that he liked the book, she wrote:

I little thought that you would care about [the poems] intrinsically as they are full of mistakes and irrelevant things that magnify the intricacy of some of them... The London Times says I represent the "latest device for concealing a lack of inspiration by means of a superficial unconventionality."

It was perhaps that kind of criticism — condemnation by a bewildered reviewer — that made her resist book publication.

The critics whose opinion Moore valued, however, supported her with telling comments. Robert McAlmon thought her poems "Poetry" and "Picking and Choosing," both statements of her aesthetic, expressed the "modern movement" to perfection. Watson at *The Dial* worried about a suitable reviewer and finally asked T. S. Eliot. In his review, Eliot suggested that Marianne Moore already had imitators, that her poetry is "too good" "to be appreciated anywhere." Pound, in the midst of his *Bel Esprit* campaign to raise funds to free Eliot from his bank job so he could write full-time, now wanted to extend the plan to bring Williams and Moore to Europe. He wrote to Harriet Monroe to nominate Moore as his first choice for the Levinson Prize, indicating that her work was truly American and modern. And Harold Latham at Macmillan suggested that Moore bring him a manuscript to consider.

By 1924, Marianne Moore had published eleven poems in *The Dial*. The Dial Press, indirectly connected with the magazine, offered to publish a book of her poems. She chose 52 poems of the 65 she had published since 1915 and four unpublished poems, arranged them in chronological order by date of composition, and added for the first time her glorious notes — references to sources for her quotations and suggestions for further reading. They were published as *Observations* and promptly won *The Dial* Award, a gift of $2,000 for service to literature during 1924. In his announcement of the award, Thayer called Moore "America's most distinguished poetess, a position held by no one," he said, "since the death of Emily Dickinson." T. S. Eliot, whose "Waste Land" had appeared in *The Dial* in 1922, was the only other poet to have received the award, the other two recipients having been Sinclair Lewis and Van Wyck Brooks. Even Ernest Hemingway (who could not get himself published in the magazine) wrote to the editors to congratulate them on their choice of Marianne Moore.

Not only did the publication of *Observations* and the championing encouragement of *The*

Dial assure Moore her first wide American readership; it also confirmed her position as a major modernist poet. Such poems as "A Grave," "New York," and "An Octopus," characterize the best of her work. A brief examination of these poems will illustrate the increased intellectual, verbal, and emotional facility Moore had developed by about 1920.

"A Grave," drafted about 1918, appeared in *The Dial* in 1921. Originally called "A Graveyard," it was rhymed, arranged in syllabic meter in three stanzas. Moore sent it to Pound for possible use in *The Little Review*. He asked: "Are you quite satisfied with the final cadence and graphic arrangement of same. . . .?" He went on to suggest she reverse the nouns in the last line and added: "Perhaps you will find a more drastic change suits you better. I do not offer an alternative as dogma or as a single and definite possibility." Whether in response to Pound's suggestion or not, Moore did make drastic changes. She stripped off part of the first stanza, altered the lineation so that every line ended after a natural phrase instead of mid-phrase or mid-word, and thereby collapsed the rhyme scheme, rendering it invisible. Never before had a poem by Marianne Moore appeared as "free verse." This unlikely precedent governed her poems from 1921 to 1925; written first in a syllabic, rhymed meter, the next thirteen poems took on the look of free verse. After the hiatus caused by her work at *The Dial*, Moore returned to her earlier verse form.

"A Grave" is a meditation on death and the sea. At the time of its composition, the shocking sinking of the *Lusitania* had just happened, and to bring matters close to home, Moore's brother had joined the Navy as a chaplain and was at sea, in wartime. For Moore, who loved the seashore and ship travel, this poem offers a dark vision of the sea which "has nothing to give but a well excavated grave." It continues,

men lower their nets, unconscious of the fact
    that they are desecrating a grave,
and row quickly away; the blades of the oars

moving together like the feet of water-spiders
    as if there were no such thing as death.
                           • • •
and the ocean, under the pulsation of light-
        houses and noise of bell-buoys,
advances as usual, looking as if it were not that
    ocean in which dropped things are bound
                                   to sink —
in which if they turn and twist, it is neither
        with volition nor consciousness.

Set against her poetry of 1915, this poem takes
a leap toward the modernity of Eliot's "The Love
Song of J. Alfred Prufrock" and Pound's "Homage
to Sextus Propertius" that her earliest work
scarcely foretold.

"New York," in *The Dial* in 1921, suggests by a
series of negative statements that the poet's new
home city is important to her not for its material-
istic advantages but for cultural opportunities.
After a catalogue of products of the wholesale fur
trade, of which New York had recently become
the largest center, set in contrast to the wilderness
on which such trade depends, Moore continues:

It is not the dime-novel exterior,
Niagara Falls, the calico horses and the
                                   war-canoe;
                           • • •
it is not the atmosphere of ingenuity,
the otter, the beaver, the puma skins
without shooting-irons or dogs;
it is not the plunder,
but "accessibility to experience."

Deftly satiric, the poem points its moral subtly,
naming business successes and elegant artifacts
without explicit judgment until, in the penulti-
mate line, they are summed up as "plunder" and
dismissed. " 'Accessibility to experience,' " instead, is the reason for admiring New York.

"An Octopus" stands as a monument to
Marianne Moore's literary vision. Occasioned by
two summers spent near Mount Rainier, Washington, it examines a natural paradise formed by
eight glaciers. On one level, the poem glistens in

admiration of the mountain's beauty and its
wealth of wild creatures, offering elaborate detail concerning plants, animals, and rock forma-
tions. On another plane, it contrasts the Christian moral code with that of ancient Greece. It is
by far Moore's longest poem and perhaps her
most profound.

An elaborate network of quotations — most of
them reworked from the originals — brings together descriptions of the mountain and of seemingly unrelated things. The following passage includes three quotations from articles about
marine life used by Moore to describe the
glaciers:

"Picking periwinkles from the cracks"
or killing prey with the concentric crushing
                           rigor of the python,
it hovers forward "spider fashion
on its arms" misleadingly like lace;
its "ghostly pallor changing
to the green metallic tinge of an
                           anemone-starred pool."

The closing lines portray the power of "the white
volcano with no weather side":

the lightning flashing at its base,
rain falling in the valleys, and snow falling
                                   on the peak —
the glassy octopus symmetrically pointed,
its claw cut by the avalanche
"with a sound like the crack of a rifle,
in a curtain of powdered snow launched like
                                   a waterfall."

These three poems, "A Grave," "New York,"
and "An Octopus," like most of the canon, are
both difficult and grand. They are tightly worded,
almost exasperating in their allusions to things
we cannot quite grasp, filled with jarring combi-
nations of images. At the same time, their majes-
ty enthralls the careful reader, offering an entry
into the poet's world where nature mirrors
humanity at its best and contradicts humanity at
its weakest.

As early as January 1924, Scofield Thayer sounded out Marianne Moore about joining *The Dial's* staff. She replied that she liked her library work and had no desire to change. In May 1925, however, she was persuaded to become acting editor, replacing Thayer who was spending more and more time abroad. Within a year, as he withdrew almost completely from the magazine, Thayer named Moore his successor.

In ten years, Moore had moved from bottom to top of the list of influential modernists. Last to be published, she became the editor of them all. *The Dial* by 1925 had achieved a circulation of 18,000 — a vastly larger circulation than other little magazines. Its contributors included the who's who among writers in America and western Europe. Although Pound, the constant gadfly, occasionally criticized its "conservatism," it published hundreds of enduringly important poems, essays, and short fiction. Moore's presence on the staff certainly added to its luster.

Moore's co-workers at *The Dial* were an interesting lot. Paul Rosenfeld wrote music criticism; Henry McBride, columnist for the *New York Sun*, critiqued modern art; and Gilbert Seldes covered the theater. Kenneth Burke, on the way to becoming *The Dial's* resident literary critic, frequented the office. Although Thayer came and went until 1927, when mental illness forced his complete break with the magazine, Watson continued to serve *The Dial* as a collaborating editor. Although in later years Moore said that she never accepted material for publication without Watson's agreement, in fact the surviving correspondence shows that she did indeed make many choices unaided. And she vigorously edited contributions.

Her editorial pen has become notorious for a few partially-told tales. One concerns Hart Crane's "Wine Menagerie," which she revised and whose title she changed to "Again." Actually, Crane expressed nothing but gratitude to her, although privately he may have protested. In another instance, she accepted a portion of Joyce's *Anna Livia Plurabelle* only to reject it later (she would have insisted Joyce cut it — an

unlikely possibility). She also turned down a group of Yeats's poems, provoking from him the query as to whether she intended to make *The Dial* reflect the "school" to which she herself belonged. And although she pared down Gertrude Stein's *Long Gay Book*, Stein seemed not to mind.

Much of what she published was superb: Bertrand Russell's "The Meaning of Meaning," Paul Valéry on Leonardo da Vinci, fiction by D. H. Lawrence and John Dos Passos, Hart Crane's "To Brooklyn Bridge," Pound's "Canto XXII," Yeats's "Among School Children," and poems by Conrad Aiken, William Carlos Williams, Louis Zukofsky, and Stanley Kunitz. Some of those whose work does not appear simply were not producing anything. For example, Wallace Stevens annually received her requests for work but had none at hand. And some writers needed fence-mending after Thayer had alienated them.

Pound was one of the latter. He had written the Paris letter in the first years of the magazine until Thayer decided to replace him with a Frenchman, Paul Morand. The change was handled badly, and when Marianne Moore asked Pound for contributions, he stormed at her, asking how she could have no inkling of how *The Dial* had mistreated him. Not only did Marianne Moore receive work from him, she promoted him for *The Dial* Award he received in 1928. Others named to receive the award during her tenure were Williams, Cummings, and Kenneth Burke.

In her position as editor, Marianne Moore wrote the monthly "Comments," two or three pages on subjects of her choice. These remarkable pieces have all the twists and turns of her poetry. In fact, in many ways they are the poems of her five years at *The Dial*; she wrote no verse between 1925 and 1930. The "Comments" cover much of the range of her poetry: books, the circus, serpents, Audubon, the Holland Tunnel. The last inspired a splendid sentence:

Our master-production, The Clifford Milburn Holland Vehicular Tunnel, is not visible. In close approach to entrance or exit it is scarcely more perceptible than a wormhole, but pourings of traffic toward Broome Street or from Canal Street indicate sand-adder selfhelpfulness within and encourage one to feel that occupancy will presently have become indigenous, i.e., that the tunnel will presently have paid for itself and be free to the public.

Where another might have written "The tunnel receives heavy use and will soon be paid for," Marianne Moore manages to bring to bear her knowledge of a particular worm's behavior by way of congratulating the city on its accomplishment and complimenting its motorists.

Some of the "Comments" included brief book reviews, but Marianne Moore's major criticism occured in her long reviews, written for *The Dial* both before and during her editorship. Early on in her relationship with the magazine, she told Gilbert Seldes, then managing editor, that she preferred to review only those books with which she had some sympathy. Inasmuch as after 1921 she was a favored reviewer and might have reviewed for *The Dial* virtually anything being published, what she chose not to write about is instructive. Such authors as Steven Vincent Benét, Edna St. Vincent Millay, Sherwood Anderson, Elinor Wylie, Laurence Houseman, and Hilda Conkling (a child poet promoted by Harriet Monroe) were all reviewed by others. Instead, she spent her energies on Eliot's *Sacred Wood*, George Moore, George Saintsbury, Thomas Hardy, E. E. Cummings, Wallace Stevens, William Carlos Williams, and Gertrude Stein.

"Well Moused, Lion," her review of Stevens's *Harmonium*, has landmark quality. Here Marianne Moore masters a master, enunciating the emerging tenets of her aesthetic: precision, gusto, and intensity. From this early essay comes a dictum she was to pursue throughout her career:

> The better the artist...the more determined he will be to set down words in such a way as to admit of no interpretation of the accent but the one intended....

She wrote about Stevens on six occasions over the years; she acted as a go-between in preparing his *Selected Poems* for Faber and Faber in 1953. She admired Stevens's work, citing the "riot of gorgeousness in which his imagination takes refuge," perhaps even preferring it to that of her other contemporaries, although her critical eye found "certain manifestations of *bravura*" "uneasy rather than bold."

While fully willing to take issue even with an author with whose work she felt some, or even great, "sympathy," she was more explicit in her censures in the "Briefer Mentions" — unsigned, one-paragraph reviews. Williams's *In the American Grain* receives praise only for the chapters on Columbus and Montezuma while Marianne Moore calls herself "unsubmissive to his pessimism and sometimes shocked by the short work he makes of decorum, verbal and other." And a review of Frances Fletcher's *A Boat of Glass* reads in its entirety:

> Liking the flowers, the icicles, "the forest's nave," and in the lines entitled "Adrift," "a boat of thin-spun glass," one wishes that each of the poems in this book were technically shipshape.

The halcyon period of *The Dial* came to an end in 1929. Since Thayer no longer had a role in the magazine, his mother had taken over his half of the deficit which mounted with inflation. Mrs. Thayer felt disinclined to support a project in which her son had no part. Watson, increasingly away from New York, could not absorb his partner's share of the funding; he decided reluctantly in the spring to discontinue the magazine with the July issue.

The Dial had a splendid decade. It triumphed during the height of the modernist period, from "The Waste Land" to Louis Zukofsky's first publications. Its dedication to *belles lettres* might not have survived the preoccupation with social concerns that marked the 1930s. Had Marianne Moore remained its editor indefinitely, she might not have carried on with her own poetry. As it happened, after a three-year delay, which included moving to Brooklyn, she again began to

20

write. Certainly, her experience as an editor contributed to the highly polished surfaces of her new work just as maturity of mind affected its content. Emboldened, perhaps, by her observation of other writers at work, she returned to the syllabic verse form of her own invention, producing such masterpieces as "The Jerboa" and "The Plumet Basilisk" in the next few years.

Confirmation

The 1930s solidified for Marianne Moore the development evidenced before 1925. A trilogy of poems — "The Steeple-Jack," "The Hero," and "The Student" — brought her work again to *Poetry*, no longer "an alien." Lincoln Kirstein's *Hound and Horn* took poetry and prose from former contributors to *The Dial*, as did Bryher's and Robert Herring's *Life and Letters To-day*. Ezra Pound, temporarily without a magazine home, turned to anthologies, giving Marianne Moore a prominent place in both *Profile* (1932) and *Active Anthology* (1933). For the former, he chose her poems from around 1919, including "Old Tiger" which he had kept without publishing for nearly fifteen years; in the latter he used only recent poems. Pound's message in *Active Anthology* is that in the work of certain authors,

> a development appears or in some cases we may say still appears to be taking place, in contra-distinction to authors in whose work no such activity has occurred or seems likely to proceed any further.

Present among those active are Williams, Eliot, Cummings, and Moore from the first generation of "new" poets. Fast at their heels are the young "objectivists," Basil Bunting, Louis Zukofsky, and George Oppen. Missing are H. D., at the time undergoing her analysis with Freud, and Stevens, never a favorite of Pound's.

Still her advocate, Pound attempted to influence Marianne Moore to replace Harriet Monroe as *Poetry's* editor. Moore replied simply that she would not want to relocate her mother in Chicago. In fact, she never again edited a magazine. From 1930 on, she supported herself by free-lance work: reviews for *Poetry* and a host of other magazines; poems accepted by *The Nation*, *Poetry*, and — after 1953 — *The New Yorker*, among many others. By 1935, another book of her poems was on the horizon. T. S. Eliot, now an editor at Faber & Faber, suggested a *Selected Poems* with an introduction by him. Macmillan agreed to bring out an American edition.

Two other books of poems, slight in length but containing some of her richest poetry, appeared in 1941 and 1944. Then there followed *Collected Poems*, brought out by both her English and American publishers in 1951. This book won for Marianne Moore the Bollingen Award, the Pulitzer Prize, and the National Book Award.

Early in the 1940s, Moore began her translation of *The Fables of La Fontaine* which was to occupy her until 1954. Her mother, always her best audience and critic, died in 1947; the translation helped her through a difficult time. After 1947, her own poetry is marked by an expanded openness of subject and language. As if to formalize the change, when preparing her *Complete Poems* in 1967, she divided the book into two sections: "Collected Poems, 1951," and "Later Poems." While the later poems are still shaped by her rigorous verse form, they now address more accessible subjects than much of the earlier work: a thoroughbred race horse, an amusement park, dancers, athletes, or writers in residence. Partly influenced by years of searching for English equivalents for La Fontaine's French, and mindful of Pound's advice to insist upon English word order — subject, predicate, object — she uses slightly less enjambed, less latinate language. Most of the mid-word rhymes disappear. Nonetheless, the later poems are fully characteristic, achieving highly nuanced meanings with such words as "unmetronomic," "adastrium," or "milkweed-witch-seed-brown."

The kind of revolutionary literary excitement which perfumed the air for the modernist poets during the 1910s and 1920s had seemed to dissipate in the 1930s. Now, they found a steadier, if occasionally embattled, acceptance from the poetry-reading public. Pound and Williams gained an untiring publisher in James Laughlin IV, whose New Directions Publishing Company was his response to Pound's instruction to "do something useful." Pound remained the hard-working promoter, but his attention wandered away from poetry toward economics during the years before his unfortunate incarceration in 1946, his remarkable *Pisan Cantos* still to appear. Williams settled into writing *Paterson*, a single poem in five books. Eliot, himself busy as a publisher, turned his attention largely to verse drama, with major exceptions like *Four Quartets*. H. D. worked at translation, drama, and fiction, but she was to make a major comeback as a poet later with her *War Trilogy*, poems flowing from her London experiences during the 1940s. Stevens, the business executive, had always participated in the revolution at a distance, although he continued to publish books of poetry. But the modernists had won their revolution. Never again could poetry retreat behind the barrier of 1912, the year of *Poetry*'s first appearance and the official beginnings of the poetry renaissance, without taking them into account.

Marianne Moore's role among them did not cease with the demise of *The Dial*. Feeling that Williams's *Adam and Eve in the City* was being neglected, she reviewed it for *The Brooklyn Daily Eagle* in 1936. She tried to help Stevens compile a book for Eliot to publish and she reviewed his work regularly. When Pound was confined at St. Elizabeth's Hospital after the war, she made many visits, providing him not only with books but also with her personal support of him as the master poet. In 1955, *Predilections*, her first book of essays and reviews, contained material from a series of talks about her contemporaries. These writings, concerning Pound, Eliot, and Stevens, give her critical judgment on their work over a thirty-year span.

Above all, for sixty years Marianne Moore wrote letters to her contemporaries. And in the replies, we learn how highly valued she had become, as person, poet, and critic. Eliot suggested, only partly teasing, that Faber should publish their correspondence. Pound's regular form of address for her was "My revered Marianna," and he counted on her to understand each cryptic reference in his letters, and to argue back, scolding him when she thought it necessary. Williams reflected upon her role when he was writing his *Autobiography:*

> She was our saint...in whom we all instinctively felt our purpose come together...like a rafter holding up the superstructure of our uncompleted building.

Ezra Pound, promoter, teacher, instigator, had the last word. Learning of Marianne Moore's death in February, 1972, he stepped out of deep silence, in which he had confined himself during the past several years, to arrange a memorial service at the Protestant Church in Venice. His tribute was to read her poem, "What Are Years? ":

> The very bird,
> grown taller as he sings, steels
> his form straight up. Though he is captive,
> his mighty singing
> says, satisfaction is a lowly
> thing, how pure a thing is joy.
> This is mortality,
> this is eternity.

Partial Chronology of Publications and Awards

1915 First professional publications in *Poetry* and *The Egoist*

1921 *Poems*

1923 *Marriage*

1924 *Observations; The Dial* Award

1935 *Selected Poems*, with an introduction by T. S. Eliot

1936 *The Pangolin and Other Verse*

1941 *What Are Years*

1944 *Nevertheless*

1945 *Rock Crystal* by Albert Stifter, translation with Elizabeth Mayer

1951 *Collected Poems;* The Bollingen Prize; The National Book Award

1952 The Pulitzer Prize

1953 National Institute of Arts and Letters, the Gold Medal for Poetry

1954 *The Fables of La Fontaine*, translation

1955 *Predilections;* elected to the American Academy of Arts and Letters

1956 *Like a Bulwark*

1958 *Idiosyncrasy and Technique; Letters to and from the Ford Motor Company*, with David Wallace

1959 *O to Be a Dragon*

1961 *A Marianne Moore Reader*

1962 *The Absentee*

1963 *Eight Poems; Puss in Boots, The Sleeping Beauty, and Cinderella*

1964 *The Arctic Ox*

1966 *Tell Me, Tell Me*

1967 *The Complete Poems of Marianne Moore* Posthumous Publications

1981 *The Complete Poems of Marianne Moore*, definitive edition

1986 *The Complete Prose of Marianne Moore*

Marianne Moore:
Vision into Verse

The Marianne Moore Collection

In 1969, Marianne Moore arranged the transfer of her literary and personal papers to the Rosenbach Museum & Library in Philadelphia. In addition, she planned a bequest to the Rosenbach of her livingroom furnishings. Upon her death in February 1972, this unusually complete collection found its permanent home.

The collection is remarkable for its inclusiveness. Most visually arresting, the living room looks almost exactly as it did in Greenwich Village, at 35 West Ninth Street, her residence since 1965. Family pieces, such as a settee and bureau from the nineteenth century, are combined with such modern items as an intricately carved coffee-table made by her friend Michael Watson, and a tiny footstool, the gift of T. S. Eliot. A painting of a yellow rose by E. E. Cummings hangs above a bookcase, as do portraits of Moore's grandparents. A secretary desk she purchased for her room at Bryn Mawr College and a small oak desk she used as editor of *The Dial* suggest the poet at work. Ornamenting the bookcases are animal-shaped figurines, baskets, Samoan wooden bowls, Venetian glass, many of them, like an elephant modeled by Malvina Hoffman, gifts intended to complement the subjects of her poems.

Books are everywhere. The library contains nearly 3,000 volumes. Not only are the books important as a list of Moore's reading; they are instructive of her method of reading itself. Most of the books have laid-in material — newspaper clippings, letters received and drafts of letters sent — chiefly to do with the books themselves. Books closely read have her own table of contents written on the back endpapers, a remarkable record of the passages of each book which were important to her. The range of the books corresponds to the range of her interests, from Jacob Abbott's classic "Rollo" stories, to a Greek grammar, dozens of volumes concerning natural history, and nearly complete collections of the works of her contemporaries, Ezra Pound, William Carlos Williams, E. E. Cummings, T. S. Eliot, and Wallace Stevens among them.

Moore retained copies of most of her own books in all their printings. In addition, first appearances of both poems and prose in magazines are present, as well as an extensive group of reviews of her work, beginning in 1916. Most of this work is supported by manuscripts, from drafts to setting copies of 192 published poems and 72 unpublished poems, as well as versions of much of the prose. These, in turn, are complemented by extensive working materials. Most informative is a series of commonplace books begun in 1907. These small notebooks are filled with notes made from both reading and conversation which Moore mined again and again for her poems. Clippings on hundreds of subjects, another history of her reading, are arranged in vertical files.

Moore was a prodigious saver of correspondence. Her collection includes letters written by and to her grandfather, beginning in 1850 when he first left home to begin his work as a Presbyterian minister. These letters are followed, chronologically, by those written by her mother to a cousin, Mary Craig Shoemaker, beginning in the 1890s — a particularly important correspondence documenting Moore's early years. When, in 1904, Moore's brother John Warner went to Yale,

The Marianne Moore Room, Rosenbach Museum & Library

Moore began her lifelong correspondence with him, broken only during vacations when he was at home, and during the two years when she and her mother lived with him in Chatham, New Jersey, 1916-1918. During the time Moore attended Bryn Mawr College, 1905-1909, the Moores wrote round-robin letters, a three-way chronicle of their activities. As in the case of the Shoemaker letters, those sent by Moore and her mother were eventually returned to Moore by the recipient.

More than 3,000 correspondents are represented in the collection, along with many of Moore's drafts or carbon copies of her letters. Correspondence with other writers is particularly rich, since Moore wrote to H. D., Ezra Pound, William Carlos Williams, T. S. Eliot, and E. E. Cummings throughout their careers. Writers of a later generation, such as Elizabeth Bishop, are also represented, as are such artists as Malvina Hoffman and Joseph Cornell. Several large collections of Moore's letters have been given to the Rosenbach by her correspondents.

Portrait photographs of Moore, from *cartes de visite* showing her as an infant to the famous cape and tricorne hat studies of the 1950s, offer examples of the work of such well-known artists as George Platt Lynes, Cecil Beaton, Richard Avedon, Lotte Jacobi, Berenice Abbott, and Henri Cartier-Bresson. Snapshots taken by Moore document trips to England and to the Northwest as well as scenes near her home in Carlisle, Pennsylvania.

The collection contains other notable material, such as daily appointment books from 1920-1969, address books, including the official one used at *The Dial*, more than a hundred watercolor and pencil sketches by Moore, and a group of drawings and paintings by contemporary artists. In addition, there are household and personal effects, from the miniature knives Moore celebrated in an essay to the trademark tricorne itself.

The Poet at Work

This remarkable collection documents Moore and her role in literary history. Likewise, it serves as the most significant resource for the exploration of her poetry, offering not only sources for the poems but also examples of her working method. With regard to the inspiration for a poem, Moore declared in 1925:

An attitude, physical or mental — a thought suggested by reading or in conversation — recurs with insistence. A few words coincident with the initial suggestion, suggest other words. Upon scrutiny, these words seem to have distorted the concept. The effort to effect a unit — in this case a poem — is perhaps abandoned. If the original, propelling sentiment reasserts itself with sufficient liveliness, a truer progress almost invariably accompanies it; and associated detail, adding impact to the concept, precipitates an acceptable development. To illustrate: a suit of armor is impressively poetic. The movable plates suggest the wearer; one is reminded of the armadillo and recalls the beauty of the ancient testudo. The idea of conflict, however, counteracts that of romance, and the subject is abandoned. However, the image lingers. Presently one encounters the iguana and is startled by the paradox of its docility in conjunction with its horrific aspect. The concept has been revived — of an armor in which beauty outweighs the thought of painful self-protectiveness. The emended theme compels development.[1]

Because of the collection, we are able to witness this complex development of a poem at first hand. The poem for which the most extensive record survives is "An Octopus," written during 1923 and 1924. While the available history of that poem is far too long to detail here, some examples suggest the process of composition.

"An Octopus" had its genesis in a trip to Mt. Rainier, Washington, in the summer of 1922. An important time of family reunion for the Moores, the visit to the Northwest was repeated the following year. Along the route by train through the

Canadian Rockies, Moore bought photographic postcards of the mountain scenery and wildlife, later writing back to a particular newsstand to purchase additional cards. On Mt. Rainier itself, where they spent the night at Paradise Lodge, Moore took snapshots of alpine wildflowers and the Nisqually Glacier. She and her brother hiked to the ice caves, posing with other climbers for a group picture. She acquired the handbook for Mt. Rainier National Park prepared by the Department of the Interior.

With these materials in hand, Moore began work on a poem. At first, as we see from the notebook in which the poem is drafted, she contemplated a poem about paradise and Adam's fall from grace. This stage of the poem combined comments about marriage and the ice-capped mountain. At some point early in 1923, Moore divided these elements and began to compose "Marriage," her long poem including the lines "I wonder what Adam and Eve/think of it by this time." Later in the spring, as we learn from a letter to her brother, she took up the subject of Mt. Rainier at the same time that she was reading John Henry Newman's *Historical Sketches*, a resource later to have a place in the poem. Working again in her notebook, she moved material discarded from "Marriage" into the notes for the new poem, drawing on her reading of *The Saints' Everlasting Rest*, by Richard Baxter, a seventeenth-century Protestant divine whose work, as we learn from a letter of 1915, had long been of interest to her. Trial beginnings and endings for the poem followed, the opening and closing lines remaining nearly constant during the long process of composition.

After these efforts, Moore stopped writing and went in search of other resources. In the same notebook, she recorded her reading in two books from which she drew a great deal of her imagery

[1]In *Everyman's Genius*, by Mary Austin. New York: Bobbs Merrill, 1925. Reprinted in *The Complete Prose of Marianne Moore*. New York: Elisabeth Sifton/Viking, 1986, p. 643.

for the poem, Walter Dwight Wilcox's *The Rockies of Canada*, a profusely illustrated account of explorations in Western Canada, and Clifton Johnson's *What to See in America*, a state-by-state travel book. Next, she circled phrases from these notes which she would use in the poem and added other phrases from the Mt. Rainier handbook. In addition, she examined her reading notebooks for descriptions taken from the *London Graphic* and the *Illustrated London News*, among many others, choosing such seemingly unrelated ideas as an inventor's desire for "glass that will bend" and a science writer's discussion of cuttlefish.

After this extensive record of the beginning of "An Octopus," its history comes to an abrupt halt until the finished poem is sent to *The Dial* in September, 1924. We learn only that the badger she had mentioned in the poem was changed, at the suggestion of James Sibley Watson, Jr., co-publisher of the magazine, to a marmot, for greater accuracy.

Other poems with much less demonstrable pre-history show what happened next. Typically, Moore made a list of phrases she might use, drawing circles around words that rhymed and linking pairs with a line. Next, she constructed the first stanza, usually a single sentence with two or three rhymed lines. At this point, even a master of her own verse form like Moore must have experienced difficulty, because succeeding stanzas had to match the first in both the number of syllables in each line and the position of the rhymes. In addition, the overriding rhythm had to remain that of speech with the accents of prose. When the poem reached a stage that pleased her, she turned to the typewriter, often making multiple carbons of a draft. Each carbon was an opportunity for revision, some bearing signs of six or seven reworkings with different colored inks and pencils. Colored pencils had another role: Moore often marked her "a," "b," and other rhymes with different colors to facilitate proper repetition of the pattern throughout a poem.

Moore's own description of her verse form and rhythm is instructive:

> I tend to write in a patterned arrangement, with rhymes; stanza as it follows stanza being identical in number of syllables and rhyme plan, with the first stanza. (Regarding the stanza as the unit, rather than the line, I sometimes divide a word at the end of a line, relying on a general straightforwardness of treatment to counteract the mannered effect.) I have a liking for the long syllables followed by three (or more) short syllables, — "lying on the air there is a bird," and for the inconspicuous or light rhyme, — "let" in flageolet, for instance, being rhymed with "set" in the lines,
>
> > Its leaps should be set
> > to the flageolet.
>
> I try to secure an effect of flowing continuity.... I am against the stock phrase and an easier use of words in verse than would be tolerated in prose. I feel that the form is the outward equivalent of a determing inner conviction, and that the rhythm is the person.[2]

In her effort to master that form, Moore was well known as a reviser, even to the extent of correcting her poems in books presented to her for signing. The process was an ongoing one, as she revised some poems for nearly every successive appearance in her books. Usually, revision took the form of deletion. For example, a long catalogue of alpine flowers was removed from "An Octopus" for her *Collected Poems* in 1951. Other poems, such as "Peter" (1925), remained fixed until 1967 when she reworked them for *Complete Poems*. In this instance, the removal of nonessential words for the sake of compression resulted in a broken pattern; consequently Moore put aside her syllabic verse form and wrote out the poem as if it were free verse with no stanzaic divisions. Although her verse form was intentionally stringent, the poems, as her revisions show, remained fluid, always open to change and ready for the artist's touch.

[2]In *The Oxford Anthology of American Literature*, edited by William Rose Benét and Norman Holmes Pearson. New York: Oxford University Press, 1938. Reprinted in *The Complete Prose of Marianne Moore*. New York: Elisabeth Sifton/Viking, 1986, pp. 644-45.

The Exhibition

The poems in the exhibition "Marianne Moore: Vision into Verse" were chosen to show the poet's transformation of visual images into poetic images. They are poems in which visual images play an important part, and their composition is documented by archival materials. In each case, the thing which triggered an image in the poem survives in the collection. Included are such diverse objects as photographs, newspaper reproductions of paintings, a flyer advertising a ballet, a mechanical crow, and a tin of boot polish. Documentation takes various forms, including notebooks, sketchbooks, newspaper and magazine clippings, and letters. The poems themselves are presented in manuscripts and Moore's own copies of her books.

As Marianne Moore emphasized in her description of the way a poem began for her, something like a suit of armor caught her attention and suggested visual connections, like an armadillo and an iguana. In that instance, the armor was left behind in the museum, while the memory of it, or perhaps a newspaper photograph of other armor, renewed its importance as an image. While it is true that many of the image-suggesting objects which became important to the poems were not themselves of the take-home variety, the objects in this exhibition were actually in the poet's hands when she was writing about them.

There is wide variation in the number of visual images at work in the poems. A poem like "Charity Overcoming Envy" has its roots in a single image, in this case a Flemish millefleur tapestry portraying an allegory of virtue winning over vice. The tapestry appeared in full color on the cover of a magazine and is minutely described in the poem. "No Swan So Fine," on the other hand, depends upon the conjunction of two images, a Louis XV candelabrum seen pictured in a magazine and a newspaper photograph of Versailles. Moore set herself the task of relating the images to each other in support of a concept, the demise of grandeur. In other examples, "A Buffalo" brings together a host of cattle from different pictorial sources, and "Style" salutes an array of artists, among them a figure skater, a gypsy dancer, and a tennis champion.

For a number of the poems in the exhibition, evidence of Moore's research survives. A letter to Bell Telephone Laboratories elicited a response concerning the temperature maintained for the "Four Quartz Crystal Clocks"; postcards requested from the Hartford Fire Insurance Company confirm the number of granite columns in the portico of its headquarters, a detail needed for a note to "Pretiolae." A sketchbook contains Moore's drawing of jerboas made at the Museum of Natural History for her poem about the desert rat.

Finally, notebooks and manuscripts display the poems as works in progress. We see the trial beginning of "An Octopus" in a notebook of drafts. The multi-colored underlinings which distinguish rhyme patterns adorn the manuscript of "His Shield." Moore's own copies of first appearances of the poems in magazines and books show her poetic images in context, the finished response to her visual stimuli, vision into verse.

"Dear St. Nicklus" 1895

On Christmas Eve, 1895, Marianne Moore left a note for "St. Nicklus" in the form of a poem. The eight-year-old writer already gave promise of what was to come — light rhyme, uncapitalized lines, and a drawing to reflect her mental images of horn and doll. Just a year later, Marianne Moore's mother wrote a cousin who had sent John Warner, Marianne's brother, a poetry book for Christmas:

You would have laughed surely, could you have heard my daughter's comment that the poetry was for Warner, rather than her. She dotes on poetry to a horrible degree. I know we shall yet have a poetess in the family, and finish our days languishing in an attic (prior to the ages when posterity & future generations will be singing our praises). She is consoled by the thought that the "poetry book" is within reach....

1. Mary Warner Moore. Autograph letter signed to Mary Craig Shoemaker, December 28, 1896.

2. Child's brass horn.

3. *Marianne Moore and Her Brother, John Warner Moore.* Photograph, [*circa* 1894].

4. Marianne Moore. "St. Nicklus." Autograph manuscript, December 25, 1895.

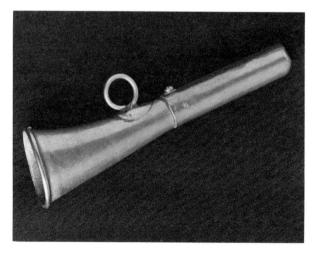

Item 2

Item 4

32

Item 3

"A Jelly-Fish" 1909

Marianne Moore's years at Bryn Mawr College, 1905-09, were marked by academic literary frustration and popular literary success. Denied access to "Major English," Moore nonetheless contributed to and became an editor of the undergraduate magazine, *Tipyn o'Bob*. Five semesters of biology were to have their effect on her poetry. For her junior year course in comparative anatomy, she drew a precise jellyfish in her laboratory notebook. Then, as a senior, she took "Imitative Writing" as an elective. Her course notebook shows that readings in seventeenth-and eighteenth-century English prose were assigned as models. In her notebook, between an assignment to write a "eulogy of any seventeenth-century man" and a comment on the imagery of Dryden ("grows more lively") is a beginning for "A Jelly-Fish":

> visible invisible
> [the] facets of a star
> an amber colored scar
> the facets of an amethyst,
> Inhabit it there are

Within a day or two, Marianne Moore wrote to her family that although she labored over her short stories, "I do seem able though, to dash off poems — ." Her poem was published in the college alumnae magazine, *The Lantern*, in June, 1909, the month of her graduation:

> Visible, invisible,
> A fluctuating charm,
> An amber-colored amethyst
> Inhabits it; your arm
> Approaches, and
> It opens and
> It closes;
> You have meant
> To catch it,
> And it shrivels;
> You abandon
> Your intent —

5. Marianne Moore. Biology laboratory notebook, 1908. (Rosenbach 1251/26)

6. Marianne Moore. Imitative Writing class notebook, 1909. (Rosenbach 1251/27)

7. Marianne Moore. "A Jelly-Fish." *O to Be a Dragon*. Viking, 1959, p. 12.

per radial c—

per radius
ad rad c + a groove
inter rad c.s
inter
ad radius
mouth
marg. lappet

gastric fils

gonads

nerve cells.

oral arms
mouth

between 1 edges of 1 arms —
Fringe of small tendrils
IS an ex and a
sub umbrella

The stomach, volum, 4 pouches
Openings in outer end of 1 St.
openings to 1 subgenital pouches — The Stom
continued out to 1 edge of the bell in numerous
Canals — six inter-rad canals dividing into
smaller — 8 ad rad sys — 4 per. rad.
Each divis of 1 stom, a gastric pouch — lining
1 pouches, 1 refer. organs — 4 gonads each
c O horse-shoe shaped etc — filaments
gastric filaments extending into 1 pouch —
gonads escape fr. 1 stom into 1 mouth —
groups of nerve cells, at 1 marg. notches

Item 5

"New York" 1921

"In 1921 New York succeeded St. Louis as the center of the wholesale fur trade," Moore tells us in her notes to "New York." A few years after her move to Greenwich Village, Moore commemorated not only her new city but also the one of her birth, as well as Allegheny City (now a part of Pittsburgh) the home of her maternal great-grandparents where she had lived for a short time.

The primary contrast in "New York" is between that great metropolis and the head of the Ohio River at Pittsburgh, formed by the confluence of the Monongahela and Allegheny Rivers — the city and the wilderness. The first images given of New York are those of furs used as clothing, such as the picardel, or Elizabethan ruff. Next come three descriptions of elegance — queen, beau, and gilt coach — from which "it is a far cry" to the "conjunction" of the two rivers in western Pennsylvania and "the scholastic philosophy of the wilderness." The poet has set up a contrast which the reader can understand, or perhaps (knowing the landscapes involved) can summon up, but with difficulty. How, one wonders, does anything near Pittsburgh suggest wilderness?

In this instance, Moore had before her a painting which had been in her family for many years. An unsigned nineteenth-century work, it depicts a mother and two children asking a blessing before their picnic lunch on the hills overlooking the Ohio River. Across the river is Allegheny City, Pennsylvania. Just down river from the scene in the painting lies the conjunction of the Monongahela and Allegheny Rivers, at the Pittsburgh point.

At the time represented in the painting, the Ohio River was the gateway to the west, the link with St. Louis and the Mississippi trade route. Between Pittsburgh and St. Louis lay the great wilderness, broken only by towns along the river. The poem suggests this landscape as a contrast to New York.

8. Artist unknown. *View of the Ohio River from above McKees Rocks.* Oil on canvas, [*circa* 1880].

9. Marianne Moore. "New York." *The Dial*, December 1921, p. 637.

Item 8

"An Octopus" 1924

In 1922, Marianne Moore made the first of two trips to Bremerton, Washington, for long summer visits with her brother. On the first trip, the family traveled up to Paradise Park on Mount Rainier for an overnight stay. Moore photographed the dramatic Nisqually Glacier and took close-ups of alpine flowers. She and her brother joined a hiking party and climbed up to the ice caves, the greatest distance visitors can reach without full climbing gear.

Back in New York, Moore began a long poem about Adam and Eve in paradise, but she was soon to divide it into "Marriage" and "An Octopus." Her working notes show her in the process of making that division, writing:

> An octopus of ice
> so cool in this the age of violence
> • • •
> one says I want to be alone
> the other also I [would] like to be alone
> why not be alone together

and further down, on the same page,

> Marriage
> with its resplendent properties

Later, the poem about Mt. Rainier emerged as a separate work:

> An Octopus
> of ice. Deceptively reserved and flat.
> it lies "in grandeur and in mass"
> beneath a sea of shifting snow-dunes;

Item 10

And the visit to the ice caves is recalled in "'grottoes from which issue penetrating draughts which make you wonder why you came.'"

10. Marianne Moore. "An Octopus" and "Marriage." Autograph draft, [1923]. (Rosenbach 1251/17)

11. *Climbers on Mount Rainier*. Photograph, [1922]. Marianne Moore and her brother John Warner Moore are third and second from the right.

12. Marianne Moore. "An Octopus." *Observations*. New York: The Dial Publishing Company, 1924, p. 83.

Item 11

"No Swan So Fine" 1932

In March 1930, Moore wrote to the English critic George Saintsbury:

The loss of your friend, Lord Balfour, must be a great one to you; for even we who knew him only as a personage, will remember his death with lasting regret. In his relations with America he was so exceedingly kind, chivalrous, and hopeful. But I myself knowing less than I ought to know about government, found it pleasant to know that Lord Balfour played a good game of tennis.

Later that year, Moore noticed a Christie's sale announcement in the *Illustrated London News*. In her notebook, she sketched one of a pair of Louis XV candelabra, "the property of the late Lord Balfour," pictured in the advertisement. When she sent the finished poem to her brother, Moore wrote:

Lord Balfour had a pair o' these candelabra which were sold last year at Christie's with his other things. Each swan has a gold saw-toothed

Item 15

THE NEW YORK TIMES MAGAZINE, MAY 10, 1931.   9

The Tapis Vert at Versailles, Where Melancholy Now Reigns as Queen.
Photo From Publishers Photo Service.

collar and chain and both feet are planted on a tree.

A year later, Moore read in the *New York Times Magazine* an article by Percy Philip, "Versailles Reborn: A Moonlight Drama." This piece was prompted by the restoration of Versailles sponsored by the Rockefeller Foundation. Philip wrote his "drama" in a fanciful vein, pretending

Item 16

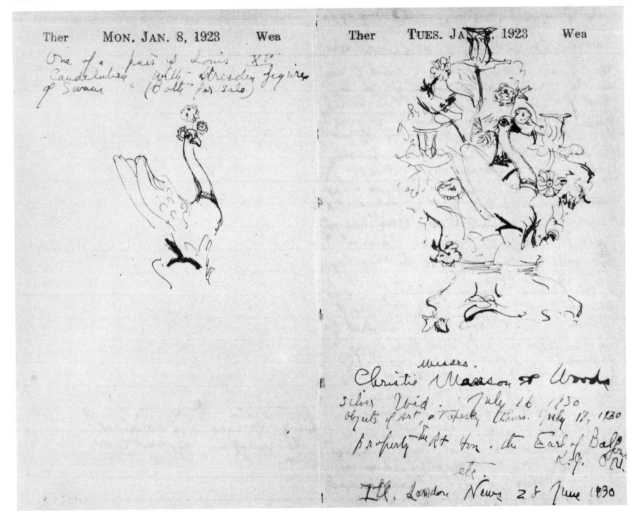

41

that the statues on the grounds protested the dullness of Versailles without the court of the Kings Louis. Moore clipped one of the accompanying pictures and wrote above it the caption from another which showed the defunct fountains, "There is no water so still as the dead fountains of Versailles."

A third element is present in the poem, one which ties in with the theme of "passing." In the same letter to her brother in which she sent the poem, Moore explains that she has written this poem for *Poetry's* twentieth anniversary number; her duty to finish it was compounded by the announcement that the magazine would probably cease publication in the spring. The impending passing of that magazine — which fortunately did not happen — would have been cause for sadness, particularly since its editor, Harriet Monroe, had welcomed Moore's work after *The Dial* ceased publication in 1929.

13. *Christies: Season 1930*. London: Constable & Company, 1930, p. 263.

14. Marianne Moore. Typed letter signed to John Warner Moore, July 31, 1932.

15. *The Tapis Vert of Versailles: Where Melancholy Reigns Supreme*. Photograph reproduced in Percy Philip, "Versailles Reborn: A Moonlight Drama," *New York Times Magazine*, May 19, 1931, p. 8.

16. Marianne Moore. *Swan Candelabrum*. Pen and ink, [1930]. (Rosenbach 1250/6)

17. Marianne Moore. "No Swan So Fine." *Active Anthology*. Edited by Ezra Pound. London: Faber and Faber, 1933, p. 206.

"The Jerboa" 1932

Life in ancient Egypt, insistently in the news in the late 1920s and early 1930s due to archaeological finds, attracted Moore's eye for the exotic artifact. "The Jerboa" weaves together dozens of references to Egyptian objects and to animals kept by the royal court, all to be set against the tiny desert rat, the "not famous" jerboa and his natural powers of survival.

The poem's first image, the great pine-cone-shaped fountain in the Vatican gardens, "passed for art" of the kind made as a gift for a "native of Thebes." In contrast as to scale, the Egyptians "liked small things," and made for children "little paired playthings/such as...ichneumon and snake," seen in a drawing Moore made in her notebook. For adults they fashioned "toilet-boxes marked/with the contents" like the ones in another drawing:

Item 18

> Lords and ladies put goose-
> grease
> paint in round bone boxes — the pivoting
> lid incised with a duck-wing
>
> or reverted duck-
> head[.]

And,

> Those who tended flower-
> beds and stables were like...
> ...the folding bedroom

made for the king's mother. This image of extravagant efficiency was inspired by a traveling bed-room of wood, brass, and gold with its golden canopy, carrying-chair, bed, and headrest. It was found in 1925 in the tomb of King Cheops' mother, Hetepheres.

These images of "too much" are set against the "abundance" of the "sand-brown jumping-rat," the jerboa, whose splendid coat needs no goose-grease to make it glow in the moonlight, and who has for a home no gold-tricked canopy but "a shining silver house/of sand." Fountains and playthings are alien to him who "lives without water, has/happiness."

18. Marianne Moore. *Toilet Boxes*. Pen and ink, [1931]. Copied from *The Illustrated London News*, November 21, 1931. (Rosenbach 1250/4)

19. Marianne Moore. *Ichneumon and Snake Toy*. Pen and ink, [*circa* 1931]. Copied from Karl Grober, *Children's Toys of Bygone Days: A History of Play-things of All Peoples from Prehistoric Times to the XIX Century* (New York: Frederich H. Stokes, 1929), p. 10. (Rosenbach 1250/5)

20. *The Folding Bedroom of Cheops' Mother, Hetepheres I*. Photograph reproduced in *The New York Times*, July 31, 1932, Rotogravure Section, p. 1.

21. *Used in the Dim Past by Some Ancient Egyptian Beauty: A Toilet-box Found at Thebes*. Photograph reproduced in *The Illustrated London News*, July 1, 1922, p. 18.

22. Marianne Moore. *Jerboas*. Pencil, 1932. Sketch made at the Museum of Natural History, New York, July 5, 1932. (Rosenbach 1253/4)

23. Marianne Moore. "The Jerboa." *Selected Poems*. London: Faber and Faber, 1935, pp. 22-23.

THE GOLDEN SLEEPING QUARTERS OF AN EGYPTIAN QUEEN WHO LIVED FIFTY CENTURIES AGO: THE PORTABLE BED CHAMBER OF QUEEN
HETEPHERES I.
the Mother of Cheops, Discovered in a Secret Tomb at Dahshur by the Harvard-Boston Expedition and Reconstructed in the Cairo Museum, Where It Now Appears as in the Above
Picture, With Its Bed and Headrest, Armchair and a Jewel Box. The Gold-Covered Panels on the Door Frames of the Chamber (Shown at Left and Right) Are Inscribed With the
Names and Titles of Her Husband, King Snefru, Who Presented the Canopy to Her.
(Times Wide World Photos.)

Item 20

Item 22

45

"*Camellia Sabina*" 1933

Things the French "keep under glass" — a jar of Bordeaux plum jam, camellias in a greenhouse, and classic wines — cluster in this poem around the notion of caretaking in the production of fruits and flowers. A book about camellias noticed at Macy's, a scholarly mongraph on camellia culture in France, an epicure's guide to France, and dozens of other stimuli affect "Camellia Sabina." A surviving source for one image is an issue of *The National Geographic* with a picture of a "mouse" — actually a rat — caught by a camera whose shutter she had tripped while taking food from the photographer's night-time wildlife table. In the poem, the description reads:

> Does yonder mouse with a
> grape in its hand and its child
> in its mouth, not portray
> the Spanish fleece suspended by the neck?

Clearly, the first two lines are derived directly from the unusual photograph, but the Spanish fleece offers an odd conjunction. The way the "mouse" holds her "child" in the photograph is certainly "by the neck" and therein lies the clue to the fleece. In the late Middle Ages, Philip IV of France founded the chivalric Order of the Golden Fleece which later spread to Spain and Austria. Still active, this organization of fifty-one knights elected from the Catholic nobility of the three countries recognizes men who have distinguished themselves by service to their fellow men. Their heraldic symbol is an oval design in which a golden lamb's fleece, draped in an arc, is suspended by the neck.

The mouse, protecting her young while taking a great risk to gather food for it, receives this honor for her heroic deed.

24. Agnes Aiken Atkinson. *Her Tail Pulled the Trigger.* Photograph reproduced in "Befriending Nature's Children," *The National Geographic Magazine*, February 1932, p. 206.

25. Marianne Moore. "Camellia Sabina." Typed manuscript [carbon], 1933. Moore sent the original to Ezra Pound for *Active Anthology*, April 5, 1933.

HER TAIL PULLED THE TRIGGER

Carrying a baby in her mouth and a grape in her right forepaw, a round-tailed wood rat took this picture when her tail caught against the flash cord as she scampered away. Because of its peculiar habit of taking things from camps and cottages and leaving other objects in their places, this rodent is sometimes known as the trade or pack rat.

Item 24

47

"The Plumet Basilisk" 1933

As by a Chinese brush, eight green
bands are painted on
    the tail — as piano keys are barred
by five black stripes across the white. This
                octave of faulty
    decorum hides the extraordinary lizard
till night-fall, which is for man the basilisk
             whose look will kill;

The plumet basilisk is the title lizard in a long
poem which compares lizard-family reptiles of
the western and eastern hemispheres. Known as
Basiliscus americanus, it inhabits Costa Rica
where "the true Chinese lizard face is found." A
newspaper photograph of a zoo keeper holding a
"rare Plumet Basilisk from Costa Rica" documents Moore's description. The caption, "Bird,
Beast or Fish? " prompted the lines

    He runs, he flies, he swims, to get to
    his basilica....

Pursuing the Asian lizard, Moore studied the
flying dragon of Malay (*Draco volans*) in an article in the February 6, 1932 issue of the *Illustrated
London News*. There W. P. Pyecraft wrote of
the frilled lizard which "refuses to be frightened"
but "deeming discretion the better part of valor,

it takes to flight. But it does not run on all fours
after the manner of the lizard tribe but runs on its
hind legs... like a sprinter."

Among her notes is a careful drawing of the
skeleton of the Malay dragon with a notation
that it has five toes and six ribs — anatomical
detail which informs the description of the
lizard, *Draco volans*:

              the smallest
dragon that knows how to dive head-first from
          a tree-top to something dry.

Floating on spread ribs,
    the boat-like body settles on the
clamshell-tinted spray sprung from the nut-
             meg tree — minute legs
    trailing half akimbo — the true divinity
of Malay.

26. *Bird, Beast, or Fish?* Photograph reproduced in
The New York Herald Tribune, January 26,
1930.

27. Marianne Moore. *Malay Dragon Skeleton*. Pen
and ink, [*circa* 1932]. (Rosenbach 1250/6)

28. Marianne Moore. "The Plumet Basilisk." *Hound
& Horn*, October/December 1933, pp. 29-34.

BIRD, BEAST OR FISH? The rare Plumet Basilisk lizard from Costa Rica, newest arrival in the London Zoo. It is brilliant green, with a plume, or fin, down its back in contrasting color.

Underwood

Item 26   *N.Y. Herald Tribune   26 Jan. 1930*

Item 27

49

"The Buffalo" 1933

A parade of animals "of ox ancestry" marches through this poem to show that the Indian buffalo "need not fear comparison" with them. In a letter to her brother, Moore discloses her intention:

I am now preparing something — in verse — about the buffalo. Not so good as Bayard Taylor I suppose, but it will be the most I can produce — in quality; comparing it with the zebu and the over-drove ox and lastly is considered, the water buffalo, as the most fiery." (August 6, 1933)

As the reference to the nineteenth-century American travel writer Bayard Taylor suggests, the

FIND IN INDIA

Seals Showing the Indian Ox, or Zebu, in All His Glory.

Item 29

animals chosen for description come from various locales.

"The Buffalo" was inspired in part by an article in the *Illustrated London News* by W. P. Pyecraft. Pyecraft says that all oxen today descend from the long extinct aurochs, a black beast with a white stripe down its back and a six-foot spread of horns, an animal which roamed over western Europe. "A beast to paint," Moore calls the aurochs, whose image survives in a picture discovered in an Augsburg shop in the nineteenth century.

Closest in appearance to the aurochs among oxen in America, John Steuart Curry's "Ajax pulling/grass — no ring/in his nose — two birds standing on his back" has long horns; because he can

Ajax, latest lithograph by John Stewart Curry on exhibition at the Ferargil Gallery

a/s. 23   1932

Item 30

be seen only in a lithograph, his back cannot be inspected for a white stripe. But Ajax grazes without a ring in his nose because he is not ferocious like the aurochs.

Other mild oxen are also found in pictures. The zebu "with white plush dewlap and warm-blooded rump" appeared in *The New York Times* in a photograph of two Indian ceramic seals "showing the Indian Ox or Zebu in all his glory." One zebu has a dewlap so long that it reaches the ground. The

> white-nosed Vermont ox yoked with its twin
>   to haul the maple sap,
> up to their knees in
>   snow

were seen in a clipping of oxen on the Coolidge farm and seem particularly placid, waiting at each tree while sap is emptied from buckets into the container they are pulling.

While fierce enough to "convert the [tiger's] fur/to harmless rubbish," the useful Indian buffalo, "albino-footed," stands "in the mud lake, with a/day's work to do," seen in another clipping showing a diorama of stuffed animals at the Field Museum of Natural History.

Six oxen are drawn from history, art, and journalism, their essentials rendered to help define and finally celebrate the Indian water buffalo and his distinguished ancestry.

29. *Seals Showing the Indian Ox, or Zebu, in All His Glory.* Photograph reproduced in *The New York Times*, November 22, 1931, p. 5

30. John Steuart Curry. *Ajax.* Lithograph, 1932. Reproduced in *Arts Weekly*, April 23, 1932, p. 161.

31. *Spring Comes to the Coolidge Farm in Vermont.* Photograph reproduced in *The New York Times*, April 3, 1933.

32. *Water Buffalo from Eastern Asia: A Group of Animals.* Photograph reproduced in *The New York Times*, April 24, 1932.

33. Marianne Moore. "The Buffalo." *Poetry*, November 1934, pp. 61-64.

SPRING COMES TO THE COOLIDGE FARM IN VERMONT.

Times Wide World Photo.

Item 31

Item 32

WATER BUFFALO FROM EASTERN ASIA: A GROUP OF ANIMALS

"Four Quartz Crystal Clocks" 1940

One of Moore's 1939 telephone bills included a flyer which described "The World's Most Accurate 'Clocks'" at the Bell Telephone Laboratories in New York. The data given in the flyer became part of "Four Quartz Crystal Clocks" in 1940. One of the facts Moore selected was that the clocks were maintained in a vault at 41 degrees centigrade; Moore translated: "the cool Bell/Laboratory time/vault." Five years later, with a passion for accuracy rivaling that of the quartz clocks, she wrote the Bell Laboratories to check the facts reported in her poem. Bell representative Paul B. Findlay replied that her statements were "accurate enough except that I would hardly call 41 degrees centigrade 'cool.'" Thereafter, Moore revised her lines to read: "the 41° Bell/Laboratory time/vault."

34. New York Bell Telephone Company. Leaflet, 1939.

35. Paul B. Findlay. Typed letter signed to Marianne Moore, April 30, 1946.

36. Marianne Moore. Autograph notes, [*circa* 1940].

37. Marianne Moore. "Four Quartz Crystal Clocks." Typed manuscript, [1940].

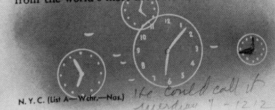

THE WORLD'S MOST ACCURATE "CLOCKS"

In the Bell Telephone Laboratories in New York, in a "time vault" whose temperature is maintained within 1/100 of a degree, at 41° centigrade, are the most accurate clocks in the world—the four quartz crystal clocks. This seemingly inanimate mineral is alive with the pulsations of time—vibrations so precise that they can be harnessed to regulate and dictate time intervals to other clocks. When properly cut and inserted in a suitable circuit, they will control the rate of electric vibration to an accuracy of one part in a million. Thus huge electric generators are paced to deliver exactly 60 cycles a second and in turn hold your electric clock to accurate time.

Again, these remarkable crystals are the master controls which regulate the frequencies of radio stations so that they will "stay put" and not stray away to spoil your favorite program.

Independently operated and checking each other for more than 10 years, these clocks are further checked with the U. S. Naval Observatory at Arlington. That's why when you call MEridian 7-1212 for correct time you get it every 15 seconds from the world's most accurate clocks.

N. Y. C. (List A—Wchr.—Nas.)

Item 34

54

"Rigorists" 1940

"We saw reindeer
browsing," a friend who'd been in Lapland,
                                    said:

                    . . .

they can run eleven
miles in fifty minutes, the feet spread when

the snow is soft,
and act as snow-shoes. They are rigorists,
however handsomely cutwork artists

of Lapland and
Siberia elaborate the trace
of saddle-girth with saw-tooth leather lace.

Item 38

IN SANTA CLAUS'S COUNTRY: TWO FAST TRAVELERS.—See Mr. Carpenter's letter.
These two reindeer ran eleven miles in 50 minutes.

The introduction of reindeer into Alaska was a story Moore knew from childhood. The Reverend Sheldon Jackson, the Presbyterian missionary who undertook the work, was the brother of a Moore family friend and an occasional visitor to Carlisle.

In the 1890s, Dr. Jackson first traveled to the Eskimo settlements of Arctic Alaska. Appalled by the conditions under which the people lived, particularly aware that their food supply was in danger, Jackson worked to make the Eskimos herders rather than hunters. He set sail for Siberia where he traded for reindeer along the coast. Finally, he was able to establish a herd among the Eskimos.

    And
this candelabrum-headed ornament
for a place where ornaments are scarce, sent

    to Alaska,
was a gift preventing the extinction
of the Eskimo. The battle was won

    by a quiet man,
Sheldon Jackson, evangel to that race
whose reprieve he read in the reindeer's face.

38. *In Santa Claus Country — Two Fast Travelers*. Photograph reproduced in *The Buffalo Express*, December 1916.

39. Marianne Moore. "Rigorists." *What Are Years?* New York: Macmillan, 1941, pp. 2-3.

"The Wood-Weasel" 1942

Moore wrote "The Wood-Weasel," a study in black and white, in February 1942 as a playful tribute to her friend Hildegarde Watson, whose name appears as the upside-down acrostic in the poem. "Wood-weasel" was the name Mrs. Watson gave the skunk, her favorite woodland

Item 40

The Famous Chilcat Blanket

By S. Hall Young, D. D.

A CHIEFTAIN'S ROBE

No proof of the Japanese origin of the Alaska Thlingets is stronger than that contained in the figures and construction of the Chilcat blanket. The history of weaving by these ingenious people is lost in the midst of antiquity, and even the significance of these strange but artistic figures, woven so deftly, is obscure.

The great white mountain goat of the northwest coast, the oldest animal of the North American Continent in point of origin, the beast of the Pliocene, furnishes the hair. This long, strong, white hair with its substratum of wooly fur, is obtained from the winter coat of this animal; then it is woven by hand. Sometimes a man, sometimes a woman, is the weaver. Various colors are weighted by bladders full of stone, and all the warp is hung upon a pole, and the woof worked in by hand needles. The blankets are very thick and firm. To give body to the warp sometimes bark is twisted in with the coarser yarn, but the cross threads are pure wool, and some of them exceedingly fine. The dyes are three: purplish black obtained from the ink-pot of the cuttle-fish, a delicate light blue from the blueberry, and an exquisite yellow from the root of the yellow cedar. The colors, with the pure white and the undyed hair, are woven into these strange figures.

Masons have professed to see in the Chilcat blanket masonic emblems, and one of their writers went so far as to try to prove by these figures that the Thlingets were descended from the ancient Jews, and practiced Masonic rites.

Thirty-five years ago these splendid blankets, sometimes eight feet across by six feet in depth including the long white fringe, sold for twenty-five or thirty dollars. Now for an inferior blanket tourists have to pay from one hundred and fifty to two hundred dollars, and even at such a price these blankets are very hard to obtain.

The splendid chieftain's robe shown in the picture could not be obtained now for less than three or four hundred dollars. These robes were handed down from uncle to nephew, and were packed in yellow cedar boxes, with great care to protect them from the moths.

The totemic figure on this robe is that of the beaver, proving the chief to belong to the grand Totem of the Crow, and the sub-Totem of the Beaver. There are also whale and crow emblems which the experienced only can detect.

There is little religious significance in these figures, as these totemic images were never objects of worship, but were emblems of the pride and glory of the family.

animal, and Moore uses it here to represent both the skunk and her friend Hildegarde Watson. In her daily diary for 1942, Moore noted on February 13th that she had compiled "material for wood-weasel!!! S. Hall Young on the famous Chilcat Blanket." This entry refers to an article by S. Hall Young in a 1916 Presbyterian missionary publication.

When in the early 1920s Moore traveled to Seattle and Vancouver, she encountered Tlingit tribal art and the Chilcat blankets. But in writing the poem, she relied on Dr. Young's article for the totemic designs and colors of the Chilcat coat. Like the coat of the wood-weasel, or skunk, the Chilcat coat is primarily black and white. Moore used it to suggest Mrs. Watson's choice of a black dress with a white gardenia as her customary formal attire. Mrs. Watson's photograph, black and white, was for many years displayed in Moore's living room bookcase.

> The inky thing
> adaptively whited with glistening
> goat-fur, is wood-warden. In his
> ermined well-cuttlefish-inked wool, he is
> determination's totem. Out-
> lawed? His sweet face and powerful feet
>   go about
>
> in chieftain's coat of Chilcat cloth.

40. S. Hall Young. "The Famous Chilcat Blanket." *Home Mission Monthly*, [May] 1916.

41. *Hildegarde Lasell Watson*. Photograph, [*circa* 1930].

42. Hildegarde Watson. Autograph letter signed to Marianne Moore, September 1, 1942.

43. Marianne Moore. "The Wood-Weasel." *The Harvard Advocate*, April 1942, p. 11.

Item 41

"The Mind is an Enchanting Thing" 1943

In a letter to Kimon Friar, Moore recalls the circumstances out of which her poem arose:

With regard to THE MIND IS AN ENCHANT-ING THING: One of the winters between 1930 and 1940, Gieseking gave at the Brooklyn Academy, a program of Handel, Bach, and Scarlatti (D.), the moral of the piece being that there is something more important than outward rightness. One doesn't get through with the fact that Herod beheaded John the Baptist, "for his oath's sake"; as he doesn't, I feel, get through with the injustice of the deaths died in the war, and in the first world war.

And in another letter, she said that the emphasis of the poem was "courage to change one's mind, willing to seem to have been wrong — unwise and improvident."

The poem explores the mind — thought, memory, heart — as a complex moral instrument. Its opening image compares the mind to

the glaze on a
katy-did wing
subdivided by sun
till the nettings are legion.

This image for the mind's beauty and complexity arises from the poet as field observer, holding a katy-did wing up to the sun.

The image which follows it turns to music, to compare the mind to "Gieseking playing Scarlatti." Here Walter Gieseking, the German pianist, is paired with the father of keyboard technique, the eighteenth-century composer Domenico Scarlatti. The two musicians share some qualities with the katy-did in the preceding image.

Scarlatti's music is remarkable for its many staccato leaps, reminiscent of the movements of a grasshopper; and Gieseking is said to have assembled the largest entomological collection in private hands.

In another image, the mind is like the

kiwi's rain-shawl
of haired feathers, the mind
feeling its way as though blind,
walks along with its eyes on the ground.

The splendid description of the kiwi suggests detailed knowledge of the kiwi's habits. On the manuscript of the poem, Moore has traced the outline of a kiwi from a tin of Kiwi brand boot polish.

Another attribute of the mind which in the finished poem reads "it's conscientious inconsistency" has its roots in a note Moore made during a lecture by Reinhold Niebuhr: "that admirable virtue, inconsistency." Near the end of the poem, this notion is reinforced and tied to the earlier mention of Scarlatti:

It's fire in the dove-neck's

iridescence; in the
inconsistencies
of Scarlatti.

44. Kiwi Boot Polish can.

45. Marianne Moore. Typed letter [carbon] to Kimon Friar, June 12, 1947.

46. Marianne Moore. "The Mind Is an Enchanting Thing." Typed manuscript, [1943].

Item 44

Marianne Moore
260 Cumberland Street
Brooklyn 5, New York

The Mind is an Enchanting Thing

is an enchanted thing
    like the glaze on a
katydid-wing
        subdivided by sun
        till the nettings are legion.
Like Gieseking playing Scarlatti;

like the apteryx-awl
    as a beak, or the
kiwi's rain-shawl
        of haired feathers, the mind
        feeling its way as though blind,
walks along with its eyes on the ground.

It has memory's ear
    that can hear without
having to hear.
        Like the gyroscope's fall,
        truly unequivocal
because trued by regnant certainty,

it is a power of
    strong enchantment. It
is like the dove-
        neck animated by
        sun; it is memory's eye;
it's conscientious inconsistency.

It tears off the veil; tears
    the temptation, the
mist the heart wears,
        from its eyes,- if the heart
        has a face; it takes apart
dejection. It's fire in the dove-neck's

irridescence, in the
    inconsistencies
of Scarlatti.
        Unconfusion submits
        its confusion to proof; it's
not a Herod's oath that cannot change.

Item 46

61

"His Shield" 1944

The pin-swin or spine-swine
    (the edgehog miscalled hedgehog) with
                all his edges out,
  echidna and echinoderm in distressed-
pin-cushion thorn-fur coats, the spiny pig
                or porcupine,
  the rhino with horned snout —
— everything is battle-dressed.

Pig-fur won't do, I'll wrap
    myself in salamander-skin like Presbyter
                John.

In the 1920s an echidna arrived at the Bronx Zoo from Australia. This spiny animal which resembles a hedgehog is called a "porcupine anteater" in Australia, according to an article Marianne Moore saw in *The New York Times*. There, the echidna is described:

Nellie is about seventeen inches long.... She looked gentle enough as she climbed up and down the wire netting that separated her from visitors. And again she looked very warlike when on the approach of fancied danger, she dropped to the floor and rolled herself up like a hedgehog.

The echidna has sharp spines. These are not only presented to the enemy but are also stuck in the ground, making it harder to lift the animal up.

The pig imagery in Moore's description of this shielded creature was prompted by the common Australian name "porcupine anteater"; the echidnoderm, a spiny sea-cucumber, and the rhino add further examples of "battle-dressed" animals.

In his
unconquerable country of unpompous
                gusto,
  gold was so common none considered it;
                greed
and flattery were unknown. Though rubies
           large as tennis-
    balls conjoined in streams so
that the mountain seemed to bleed,

the inextinguishable
  salamander styled himself but presbyter.
              His shield
was his humility.

The legend of Presbyter John is retold in a biography of Haile Selassie which Moore purchased in the 1930s. There it is explained how the fabulous "King of All the Indies" became associated with Ethiopia, confusion between the two regions having been common in Europe by the time the legend was fully-grown in the twelfth century.

Moore marked passages in the book, in particular those which describe the lavishness of the king's court and end:

Do you ask why, though ruling in such magnificence, he styles himself only "presbyter"? That is his humility.

Another passage offered examples of his wealth, ready for Moore to reshape:

His wealth came from mines so rich that the mind of man could scarce picture them. Out of a magic mountain within his territories a river of rubies flowed, the precious stones so thickly clustering that from afar it seemed the mountain bled. Gold was so common none considered it.... The king hunted not lions but dragons, protected from their breath by robes of salamander skin. In these he passed through fire to the amazement of all beholders.

This imaginary benevolent ruler, shielded by humility and his salamander-skin coat, is "flanked by household lion cubs" like Haile Selassie. The presence of the latter brings the 1944 poem to the level of a plea for the Ethiopian ruler and his beleaguered country where the Axis and Allied armies fought a major campaign in World War II.

47. "Rare Animal Freak Is Echidna in Zoo." *The New York Times*, February 19, 1922.

48. Princess Asfa Yilma. *Haile Selassie: Emperor of Ethiopia*. New York: Appleton-Century, 1936, p. 77.

49. Marianne Moore. "His Shield." Typed manuscript, [1944].

Item 47

"Voracities and Verities Sometimes Are Interacting" 1947

Moore introduced this poem during a poetry reading with this summary:

A kind of book review of Captain James Corbett's hunting tigers in India; also sour grapes I'm afraid when I say I don't like diamonds — perhaps "Voracities and Verities."

The poem begins with the latter notion:

I don't like diamonds;
the emerald's "grass-lamp glow" is better;
and unobtrusiveness is dazzling,
upon occasion.

On a copy of this poem given to her close friend Louise Crane, Moore wrote of the first line, "Said by you to me, Louise, and now by me to you." Emeralds were another matter. Moore cherished a family heirloom, a brooch made of a plain flat rectangle of onyx lit in the center by a large square emerald.

In the second stanza, Moore says

and to a tiger book I am reading —
I think you know the one —
I am under obligation.

Miss Crane had recently given her a copy of *Man-Eaters of Kumaon* by Jim Corbett. These extraordinary, true tales of Corbett's expeditions in the high Himalayas detail the "voracities" of the poem's title. From 1926 to 1930, sixty-four people had been killed by man-eating tigers in a network of tiny villages. Desperate for aid, the government called upon the noted hunter. This hair-raising book is the story of his attempt to protect the villagers and to educate his readers about tigers and their habits. The tigers' voracities, he says, arise from lack of proper food; ordinarily, they will not attack men.

The major contrasting "verity" in the poem occurs in the last two lines:

One may be pardoned, yes I know
one may, for love undying.

Moore drew her statement from the last line of the letter of Paul to the Ephesians, as evidenced by the annotation in her Bible where she has written "for love undying" on the back flyleaf. In his letter, Paul emphasizes the contrast of "the passions of our flesh" which mean that "we were by nature children of wrath." But we are saved through faith, and he tells the Ephesians to "put on the whole armor of God," an evocative passage for a poet whose armoring is so well known. He closes the letter: "Grace be with all who love our Lord Jesus Christ with love undying." Expressed in the poem is Jim Corbett's selfless love for his fellow men, his verity interacting with the voracity of the tigers which, thwarted in their quest for food by the encroachment of men, exercise their wrath upon them. As the manuscript makes clear, Moore's deep affection for a friend is another verity brought to mind by her friend's generosity.

50. Jim Corbett. *Man-Eaters of Kumaon*. New York: Oxford University Press, 1946.

51. *The New Testament*. Revised Standard Version. New York: Thomas Nelson and Sons, 1946.

52. Onyx and emerald brooch. Engraved with the name of Sallie Eyster.

53. Marianne Moore. "Voracities and Verities Sometimes Are Interacting." *Quarterly Review of Literature*, 1948, p. 124.

Item 52

Item 50

"Pretiolae" 1950

The dutiful, the firemen of Hartford,
Are not without a reward—
A temple of Apollo on a velvet sward

And legend has it that small pretzels come,
Not from Reading but from Rome:
A suppliant's folded arms twisted by a thumb.

NOTE

The Hartford Fire Insurance Company and
Hartford Accident and Indemnity Company
building — 690 Asylum Avenue, Hartford, Con-
necticut — as part of its classic facade, has six
granite columns supporting the pediment; all of
solid granite.

Item 54

66

Pretiolae are thought by the *New York Times* to have been originally Roman — little pieces of baked dough symbolizing the folded arms of a suppliant, presented to children for dutifully said prayers. "Little Pretzels" were introduced to America in the 18th Century from Germany, by bakeries in Lititz and Reading, Pennsylvania, in accordance with a secret recipe — hand-twisted for factory ovens.

This uncollected poem appeared in the Harvard *Wake* and commemorates an impromptu visit Moore and her brother made to Wallace Stevens at his office at the Hartford Insurance Companies where he was a vice-president. The visit, while a success, was a bit stiff with Stevens piloting his visitors around the forbiddingly solid building.

Moore's research for the poem included a letter to the company to inquire the precise number of columns in the facade. The response included postcards offering three views of the building. Clearly, the Apollo of the temple refers to Stevens who kept a private file for his poetry in his office. And when writing the poem, Moore had before her a clipping showing firemen at work amid great danger.

Not so obvious is the reference to pretzels. Inspired by an article in the *New York Times* concerning the origin of the pretzel, Moore made the connection with Stevens, who was born in Reading, the home of the first pretzels in America. At the time, Moore was engaged in helping Stevens to prepare his *Collected Poems* for Faber and Faber.

54. *Facade of the Hartford Fire Insurance Company Headquarters*. Postcard, n.d.

55. Hartford Fire Insurance Company. Advertisement, n.d. Showing the Hartford Company's logo, a hart.

56. "'Pretzel Town' Turns Out to Honor Native Product." *The New York Times*, May 10, 1951.

Item 56

Y 10, 1951.

'Pretzel Town' Turns Out To Honor Native Product

By The United Press.

LITITZ, Pa., May 9—This town of 5,500 turned out today for a celebration honoring a "secret formula" that produced the first commercial pretzel.

That recipe, passed along by a vagabond to a local baker shortly after the outbreak of the Civil War, resulted in a multi-million-dollar industry that was 90 years old today.

Senator James H. Duff and Representative Paul B. Dague, both Republicans; several state officials, and residents from babes-in-arms to octogenarians joined a parade to the world's first pretzel factory.

Representatives of the industry and descendants of the first pretzel baker also were on hand when a plaque donated by the National Pretzel Bakers Institute was unveiled to the memory of Julius Sturgis, who turned out commercially the first of the salted delicacies.

57. Hartford Fire Insurance Company. Advertisement, n.d. Showing firemen at work and a policy in the name of Abraham Lincoln.

58. Ernestine R. Robins. Autograph letter signed to Marianne Moore, August 15, 1950.

59. Marianne Moore. "Pretiolae." *Wake*, 1950, p. 4.

Item 57

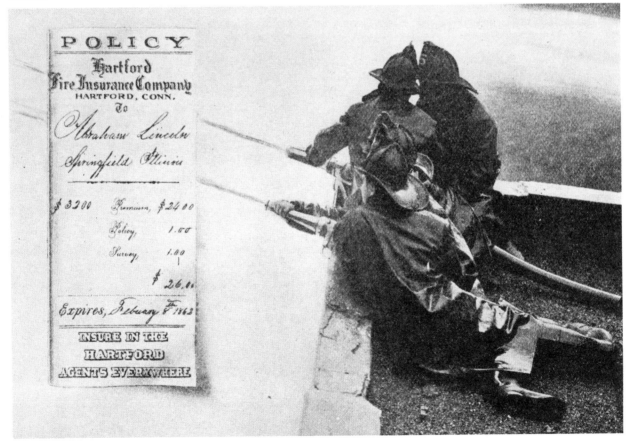

"Tom Fool at Jamaica" 1953

A poem elaborately documented by Moore's notes, this salute to jockey Ted Atkinson and his most famous mount of the 1952 racing season, Tom Fool, interweaves concerns as varied as the Spanish Civil War and the vice of gambling.

Be infallible at your peril, for your
system will fail,
and select as a model the schoolboy in Spain
who at the age of six, portrayed a mule
and jockey
who had pulled up for a snail.

Item 60

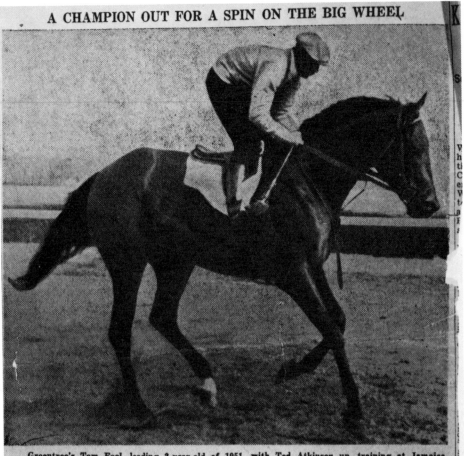

A CHAMPION OUT FOR A SPIN ON THE BIG WHEEL

Greentree's Tom Fool, leading 2-year-old of 1951, with Ted Atkinson up, training at Jamaica, where the New York racing season will start today.

Item 64

While on the subject of old-time favorites, it is worth pausing to pay respects to a Victor ten-inch revival—"Fats" Waller Favorites. "Fats," who died in 1943, was a protean jazz figure. He could write durable tunes like Ain't Misbehavin, he could tickle the

Richard Tucker (Pix)
"Fats" Waller.

ivories and he could sing with a hoarse, playful skill. His personality shines through his work on

Item 65

70

The drawing which inspired this image, part of a fund-raising effort for Republican Spain in the 1930s, shows the mule reigned in sharply to avoid an oversized snail. The quick maneuver suggests the agile Tom Fool; the circumstances of the drawing recall those of the Lippizaner dressage horses, originally in Spain, but taken to safety in Austria at the time of the war.

A host of articles about Tom Fool are quoted extensively in the poem, particularly Ted Atkinson's descriptions of the Greentree Stables' favorite as "a handy horse, one that can do things." With Atkinson up, wearing Greentree's pink and black silks as the postcard shows, "unconformity," like the horse's one white foot, keynotes the champion's personality. As his jockey said, "He was a great horse but I was fond of him not so much for what he achieved as for what he was."

The poem shifts abruptly to other champions, musical ones led up to by the sounds of the racetrack: "the harmonious rush," "centaurs' legs in tune," competing "kettledrums," "a rhapsody." Fats Waller, composer of "Ain't Misbehavin'," Ozzie Smith, the famous drummer, and Eubie Blake, the pianist known for his role in the revue *Shuffle Along,* are all jazz musicians remarkable for their "unconformity" as great improvisors.

60. Marianne Moore. *Mule and Jockey.* Pencil, n.d. A tracing of a drawing by Giulio Gomez, age 6.

61. *Ted Atkinson up on Tom Fool.* Postcard, n.d.

62. Arthur Daley. "Farewell to Flamingoes." *The New York Times,* March 3, 1952.

63. Joseph C. Nichols. "Cappy the Caller." *The New York Times,* July 24, 1952.

64. "A Champion out for a Spin on the Big Wheel." *The New York Times,* April 1, 1952.

65. Howard Taubman. "Gershwin's Girl Crazy Is Latest Revival." *The New York Times,* March 16, 1952.

66. *Shuffle Along.* Playbill, May 8, 1922.

67. Marianne Moore. "Tom Fool at Jamaica." *New Yorker,* June 13, 1953, p. 32.

"The Sycamore" 1955

Marianne Moore's inspiration for the first twelve lines of "The Sycamore" came from two magazine pictures. The first image appears in a clipping from a magazine published in 1952. "An Albino Giraffe Is Seen by Man for the First Time and Photographed in Color" is the heading of a short piece about the discovery by the Macnab-Snyder expedition in Western Kenya. Nine minutes of color film resulted, four frames of which are reproduced with the article. As shown, the giraffe is decidedly white, darkening toward the legs.

> Against a gun-metal sky
> I saw an albino giraffe. Without
> leaves to modify,
> chamois-white as
> said, though partly pied near the base,
> it towered where a chain of
> stepping-stones lay in a stream
> nearby;

The second clipping, an advertisement for feed captioned "Why Pigs Grow Big in Missouri" (the state of Moore's birth), shows Hampshire hogs and is labeled by Moore "lucky stones." The white band around the Hampshire looks similar to the stripe of white granite that occurs on dark stones called "lucky" by rock collectors.

> glamor to stir the envy
>
> of anything in motley —
> Hampshire pig, the living lucky-
> stone; or
> all-white butterfly.
> A commonplace:
> there's more than just one kind of grace.

The exotic white giraffe and the common Hampshire pig, while showing different kinds of grace, are united in that the giraffe is "partly pied" and the pig wears "motley." The unique and the

Item 68

72

everyday, the wild and the domestic, are nature's contrasts which the poem resolves into a single "commonplace."

68. "An Albino Giraffe Is Seen by Man for the First Time and Photographed in Color." [*Life* ?], [*circa* 1952].

69. Penn Chemicals. "Why Pigs Grow Big in Missouri." Advertisement, in *Time*, November 13, 1950, p. 114.

70. A lucky stone.

71. Marianne Moore. "The Sycamore." *Like a Bulwark*. New York: Viking, 1957, p. 17.

Item 69

Why pigs grow big in Missouri

"Style" 1956

In her 1955 appointment book, Moore quotes Janet Flanner quoting André Malraux in the *New Yorker*: "Art: that whereby forms are transmuted into style." Evidence of four artists of style commemorated in this poem is present in Moore's papers and notebooks.

The first named, Vincente Escudero, is the 62-year-old Gypsy flamenco dancer whom Moore had seen perform in February 1955. He had last toured this country in 1935, before the Spanish Civil War. Moore made notes after the performance, beginning with a description of "the hair fine crescent moon over the roofs of S. Oxford Street" observed on her route to the subway for Manhattan. This observation she applied to the dancer himself:

STYLE

revives in Escudero's constant of the
                                    plumbline,
axis of the hair-fine moon — his counter
                        camber of the skater.
No more fanatical adjuster
            of the tilted hat
        than Escudero;
                ...
the traditional unwavy
            Sandeman sailor
    is Escudero's;

The tilted hat is a distillation of her notes: "The stately elegance, the Sandeman sailor which he would tilt, tilt a little differently, tilt again and lower at the left."

The next two gentlemen of style pair a figure skater and a tennis player:

And we — besides evolving
    the classic silhouette, Dick Button
                        whittled slender —
have an Iberian-American champion yet,
the deadly Etchebaster.
                ...
Etchebaster's art, his catlike ease, his
                        mousing pose,
his genius for anticipatory tactics,
    preclude envy....

Item 72

Both the figure skater Dick Button and the tennis player Pierre Etchebaster had long reigns as champions. Button won two Olympic gold medals and five world championships; Etchebaster retired at 60 after holding the court tennis open championship for 36 years. For the latter, "deadly" is a compliment, meant to condense the following remark by Allison Danzig in *The New York Times*: "[Compared to the previous champion, Jay Gould,] his play on the floor had the same combination of strength and delicacy, the same deadly accuracy in cutting the cloth ball down for unbeatable chases that is the acme of artistry with a racquet."

The last artist named in the poem is also reflected in Moore's notebooks. Rosario Escudero, a guitarist with Vincente Escudero's company "but not related to him," plays "lingering hand and wrist—dangling out the notes or playing faster and faster as blades of a fan gather speed." Moore rephrased her note for the poem:

> the guitar, Rosario's —
> wrist-rest for a dangling hand
> that's suddenly set humming fast fast fast
> and faster.

There are other models of style in the poem — Casals, another Spanish dancer, Soledad, Palestrina, and El Greco. They, with the four named above, transmuted their forms — dance, music, painting, and sport — into style.

72. "Vicente Escudero, Gypsy Dancer, Is Due at Playhouse Feb. 7 after Long Absence." *The New York Times*, January 13, 1955.

73. *Vicente Escudero's Spanish Dancers and Musicians.* Playbill, February 26, 1955.

74. Allison Danzig. "Unbeaten Etchebaster, 60, Ends Reign over Court Tennis World." *The New York Times*, February 13, 1954.

75. Arthur Daley. "Success Came on Steel." *The New York Times*, January 2, 1956.

76. Marianne Moore. Autograph notes, [*circa* 1955]. (Rosenbach 1251/19)

77. Marianne Moore, "Style." Typed manuscript, [1956].

Item 74

"Blessed Is the Man" 1956

(Ah, Giorgione! there are those who
                                    mongrelize
and those who heighten anything they
                    touch; although it may well be
that if Giorgione's self-portrait were not
                                    said to be he,
it might not take my fancy. Blessed the
                                    geniuses who know

that egomania is not a duty.)

The sixteenth-century Venetian painter Giorgione was featured in *Life* at the time of an exhibition of his work in Venice. A genius who died at 33, Giorgione left behind from two to seventy works — depending on critics' attributions. Even the few paintings with firm attributions are unsigned. His self-portrait, which exists only in a seventeenth-century copy, attracted Moore to this old master who knew "that egomania is not a duty."

James B. Conant, former president of Harvard and in 1956 Ambassador to Germany, published *The Citadel of Learning* at the time Moore was working on her poem. Reviewed by Charles Poore in *The New York Times*, his book tackles the state of higher education in America with rhetoric common to the Cold War era:

> We in the free world, through our schools, colleges, and universities seek to perpetuate that tradition of Western culture which emphasizes diversity, controversy and tolerance. The Soviets seek uniformity and strict adherence to the creed of Marxism-Leninism.

As Charles Poore remarks of this stance, comparing Conant to Lincoln,

Some of his suggestions will tend...toward stirring choler. Yet, like an earlier advocate of emancipation, he does not equivocate, he does not excuse, he will not retreat and he will be heard.

In her copy of this review, Moore underlined both passages for use in her poem in these lines:

"Diversity, controversy; tolerance" — in that
                                    "citadel
of learning" we have a fort that ought to
                                    armor us well.

Item 78

76

Books of The Times

By CHARLES POORE

"THE CITADEL OF LEARNING,"* by James Bryant Conant, is certainly the most stimulating and will, I hope, be one of the most influential discussions of education in the clamorous world we know. He can be blunt and suave in the same sentence and he is always persuasive.

Not all that he proposes will raise enough hallelujahs among American educator-crackers to make a chorale. Some of his suggestions, indeed, will tend more toward stirring choler. Yet, like an earlier advocate of emancipation, he does not equivocate, he does not excuse, he will not retreat and he will be heard.

As you know, Dr. Conant is a distinguished scientist, a former president of Harvard, a veteran of the Washington bureaucratic wars, a recent High Commissioner for Germany and now our Ambassador there. He takes his text from some words until recently ascribed to Stalin and now, doubtless, assigned to the collective thinking of the totalitarian mind. Freely translated it runs:

"In front of us stands the citadel of learning. This citadel we must capture at any price. This citadel must be taken by our

Harvard Yard

Item 79

A later passage in the poem takes on writers:

> Brazen authors, downright soiled and
> downright spoiled, as if sound
> and exceptional, are the old quasi-modish
> counterfeit,
> *mitin*-proofing conscience against character.

Although her note identifies "mitin" as a word derived from the French "la mite" (moth) and as a moth-proofing chemical, there is more to its story, lending even more force. It is the one moth repellant which becomes part of the fabric itself — actually dyed in the wool — rather than applied externally as a preventive. A mitin-proofed conscience is, thereby, likely to be permanent.

77

78. "The Mystery of an Old Master." *Life*, October 24, 1955.

79. Charles Poore. "Books of the Times." *The New York Times*, April 7, 1956, p. 17.

80. Alexander R. Hammer. "Spring Cleaning Time Is Near, Rise in Moth Ball Sales Shows." *The New York Times*, April 7, 1956.

81. Geigy Chemical Corporation. "Mitin." Advertisement, n.d.

82. Marianne Moore. "Blessed Is the Man." *Ladies Home Journal*, August 1956, p. 101.

Item 80

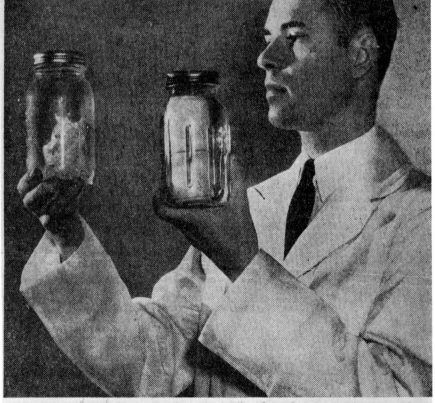

HELD IN EVIDENCE: Researcher Don Ott at Geigy shows damage moth grubs, or larvae, can cause to woolens in six weeks. Cloth in jar at left is reduced to shreds and larvae still live. Cloth in jar at right is treated with Mitin which killed larvae and saved fabric.

"Saint Nicholas" 1958

SAINT NICHOLAS

might I, if you can find it, be given
a chameleon with tail
that curls like a watch spring; and vertical
on the body — including the face — pale
tiger-stripes, about seven;
    (the melanin in the skin
      having been shaded from the sun by thin
        bars; the spinal dome
          beaded along the ridge
        as if it were platinum)?

Moore's note to "Saint Nicholas" tells us where to look for the chameleon portrayed in the first stanza: "See photograph in Life, September 15, 1958, with a letter from Dr. Doris Cochran, curator of reptiles and amphibians, National Museum, Washington, D.C." Dr. Cochran had responded to an article, "Freckles: Why Do They Come? " and she explained that melanin, which causes tan in human skin, is found also in most vertebrates. She offered as an example the photograph of a chameleon darkened by exposure to light except where its cage bars had cast shadows. Long interested in both chameleons and protective coloration, Moore transformed this photograph into a wished-for Christmas gift.

In a letter to her friend Barbara Church, the first three paragraphs refer to Moore's poem "Saint Nicholas," written between September and December 1985. In September 1958, Barbara Church had sent Moore a postcard of Hans von Marées' painting of Saint Hubert with a stag. Moore thanked her, commenting that Hans von Marées

died the year I was born. Now "one of my favorites" although this is the first of his paintings I have seen. The spirit is beyond words — makes comment, coarse — the hand, the foot, the head. And the natural, incomparably accurate dog with paws crossed, his head looking far away from his master, — just panting.

Item 83

79

Moore sent a draft of the poem to Mrs. Church and marked the section on Saint Hubert with brackets, adding in the margin: "The Munich post-card, Barbara." The original painting, "Der heilige Hubertus," is part of a triptych, "Die drei Reiter," painted between 1885 and 1887 and now in Munich. Between the stag's antlers, which are decorated with lighted tapers, stands a figure of Christ, the "stag with a Figure entined" of the poem.

83. Hans von Marées. *Der heilige Hubertus.* Oil on canvas, 1885-87. Photograph of a published reproduction.

84. Marianne Moore. Autograph letter signed to Barbara Church, September 12, 1958.

85. "Letter to the Editor." *Life,* September 15, 1958.

86. Marianne Moore. "St. Nicholas." Typed manuscript, 1958.

Item 85

CHAMELEON SHOWING EFFECTS OF MELANIN

80

"No Better Than a 'Withered Daffodil' " 1959

This short poem recounts a movement from momentary sadness to joy, drawing on images suggested by Ben Jonson and Sir Philip Sidney.

NO BETTER THAN
A "WITHERED DAFFODIL"

Ben Jonson said he was? "O I could still
like melting snow upon some craggy hill,
    drop, drop, drop, drop."

I too until I saw that French brocade
blaze green as though some lizard in the shade
    became exact —

set off by replicas of violet —
like Sidney, leaning in his striped jacket
    against a lime —

a work of art. And I too seemed to be
an insouciant rester by a tree —
    no daffodil.

Jonson's contribution is a poem from *Cynthia's Revels*. The poem begins "Slow, slow, fresh fount, keep time with my salt tears," the lament of Echo upon the death of Narcissus. Echo's state of mind is given in the quotation which opens Jonson's poem and ends, "Since nature's pride is now a withered daffodil." Echo's language should tip us off to the satire even if we do not know that Jonson's comedy is a satire on the Elizabethan court.

The French brocade which lifted the speaker above thoughts like Echo's is the fabric of a majestic jacket Moore wore on special occasions. Its iridescent greens and violets change with the light, prompting Moore's characteristic allusion to a lizard which "became exact."

A handsome book of Elizabethan miniatures reveals a portrait of Sidney, resplendently garbed, debonair and carefree, the "insouciant rester" against a lime tree.

Item 87

81

87. Isaac Oliver. *Unknown Melancholy Young Man* (formerly identified as Sir Philip Sidney). Watercolor, n.d. Reproduced in Carl Winter, *Elizabethan Miniatures* (London: King Penguin Books, 1943), Plate VIII.

88. Ben Jonson. "Slow, Slow, Fresh Fount," from *Cynthia's Revels. The Queen's Garland.* Edited by FitzRoy Carrington. New York: R. H. Russell, 1900, p. 88.

89. A brocade jacket.

90. *Marianne Moore Wearing a Brocade Jacket.* Photograph, [*circa* 1964]. Marianne Moore is seated in her living room.

91. Marianne Moore. "No Better than a 'Withered Daffodil.' " *Art News*, March 1959, p. 44.

"Leonardo da Vinci's" 1959

From the Vatican through the offices of *Time* came Leonardo da Vinci's unfinished masterpiece, *St. Jerome*, to the poet who knew well the story of St. Jerome's translation of the Vulgate and who particularly admired lions. The painting appears in the first stanza of the poem:

Item 92

"ST. JEROME," AN UNFINISHED PICTURE BY LEONARDO DA VINCI, IS AMONG THE VATICAN'S CHIEF TREASURES

83

LEONARDO DA VINCI'S

Saint Jerome and his lion
　　in that hermitage
of walls half gone,
　　　share sanctuary for a sage —
joint-frame for impassioned ingenious
　　　Jerome versed in language —
and for a lion like one on the skin of which
　　　Hercules' club made no impression.

St. Jerome's lion points to the final image in the
poem, Haile Selassie, who kept a dozen lions at
his palace. The king of beasts was a symbol of
kingship for this young emperor whose priorities
Moore admired: education, communication,
and employment for all Ethiopians. She salutes
him along with Leonardo's painting:

　　　Blaze on, picture,
saint, beast; and Lion Haile Selassie, with
　　　　　　　　　　　　　　household
　　lions as symbol of sovereignty.

Item 93

92. " 'St. Jerome,' an Unfinished Picture by Leonardo
da Vinci, Is among the Vatican's Chief Treasures."
Time, May 18, 1959, p. 73.

93. *Haile Selassie.* Reproduction of a photograph in
[*Time*?], n. d.

94. Marianne Moore. "Haile Selassie: 3 Priorities."
Autograph note, August 12, 1950.

95. Marianne Moore. "Leonardo da Vinci's." *New
Yorker*, July 18, 1959, p. 22.

"To Victor Hugo of My Crow Pluto" 1961

Asked for a contribution by *Harper's Bazaar*, Moore wrote her only prose fantasy, "My Crow Pluto." In that brief sketch, she described a pet crow who had adopted her and who often helped her with small tasks, such as fetching her pocket-sized dictionary. In a companion poem, she celebrates the same crow, in reality a wind-up toy of painted metal which could walk and flap its wings.

The last verse of a poem by Victor Hugo suggested an epigraph to Moore. As an old clipping gives the text of the verse:

> *Soyez comme l'oiseau posé pour un instant*
> *Sur des rameux trop frêles*
> *Qui sent ployer la branche et qui chant*
>   *pourtant,*
> *Sachant qu'il a des ailes!*

Moore chose to revamp the meaning of the last lines slightly for her epigraph. Instead of the "bird perched for an instant on a branch who, feeling movement beneath him, still sings, knowing that he has wings," she writes: " 'Even when the bird is walking we know that it has wings.' "

The poem is an experiment in vowel sounds and short lines which engages in "esperanto madinusa" Italianate words to describe the crow:

> my crow
> Pluto,
>
> the true
> Plato,
>
> azzuro-
> negro

green-blue
rainbow —

96. Mechanical crow. German, n.d.

97. "He Has Wings." *The New York Times*, March 20, 1932.

98. Marianne Moore. "To Victor Hugo of My Crow Pluto." Autograph manuscript, [1961].

99. Marianne Moore. "To Victor Hugo of My Crow Pluto." Typed manuscript, [1961].

100. Marianne Moore. "To Victor Hugo of My Crow Pluto." *Harper's Bazaar*, October 1961, p. 185.

Item 96

"Arthur Mitchell" 1962

Arthur Mitchell, one of the great soloists with the New York City Ballet, danced the role of Puck in *A Mid-Summer Night's Dream*. Lincoln Kirstein, president of the Ballet, asked Moore for a contribution to use in the souvenir program for the 1962 season. Having in mind Mitchell costumed as a dragonfly, she wrote a nine-line poem which has the speed and brilliant color of Mitchell in his virtuoso performance.

> Slim dragonfly
> too rapid for the eye
>   to cage —

contagious gem of virtuosity —
make visible, mentality.
Your jewels of mobility

> reveal
>   and veil
>   a peacock-tail.

101. The New York City Ballet. Subscription form, 1965.

102. Marianne Moore. Typed letter signed to Lincoln Kirstein, October 31, 1961 and November 1, 1961.

Item 101

NEW YORK STATE THEATER, *Lincoln Center,*

"Charity Overcoming Envy" 1963

Marianne Moore created "Charity Overcoming Envy" in response to pictures of a tapestry in the Burrell Collection at the Glasgow Art Gallery and Museum. Having been given a postcard of the tapestry by Lawrence Scott in January 1962, she sent to the museum for more cards and received in addition two booklets.

One of the items sent was a copy of *The Scottish Review*. In it, William Wells discusses the tapestry on pages 7-9 as a fifteenth-century depiction of the popular Psychomachia of Prudentius, a fifth-century allegory which portrays the conflict between the virtues and the vices. From Wells's article, Moore took many phrases for her notes, choosing for the poem "mosaic of flowers" and "not rooted." She adapted two other phrases from the article: flowers "massed together" become "bunched together" (quotation marks used despite the change of wording); and "chain-armour" becomes "chest armor over chain mail" (without quotation marks in the poem). It appears that only these four borrowings made their way into the poem. Always the scientific observer, Moore examined the color print of the tapestry for the rest of her description. She shows her reader the millefleur tapestry with precision: the "little flattened out/sunflowers" are those above Envy's right arm. She portrays the figures in their relative positions and attitudes: Envy "crouching uneasily," "cowering away" from Charity, looking up at the elephant. While the figures in the tapestry suggest a narrative, the "story" Moore creates for them is entirely her own invention. A notebook entry offers the crux of the story she first proposed: "Charity has a problem — how to preserve itself and to learn patience,

the...mastery is from within." Ultimately, she drew together Charity's conflict and Envy's self-pity into a single "insupportably tiring" problem to which she could apply the same deliverance: "The Gordian knot need not be cut."

103. *Charity Overcoming Envy*. Tapestry, Flemish, 15th century. Reproduced in *The Scottish Review*, 1957, cover illustration.

104. Marianne Moore. Typed letter signed to the Glasgow Museum and Art Galleries, March 28, 1962.

105. Marianne Moore. "Charity Overcoming Envy." Typed manuscript, 1962.

Item 103

87

" 'Avec Ardeur' " 1963

Like her poem on the crow Pluto, this poem is an experiment in the short line — a serious departure for a poet whose lines were frequently too long for the octavo format of her books. Like the earlier poem, it too is light-hearted with several serious statements embedded beneath the playfulness.

While it is concerned chiefly with language, it displays one concrete image:

> Though flat
> myself, I'd say that
>
> "Atlas"
> (pressed glass)
>
> looks best
> embossed.

Here is the classic canning jar, its prominent name far more striking than those on "Mason" or "Ball" jars, and a name meant to suggest survival of the most rugged canning practices.

The poem went through several changes of title. The first, supplied by Lawrence Scott who first printed it at Harvard, arose from Scott's having typed out the poem on Lowell House stationery. The apparently title-less poem appeared below the Lowell House motto, "Occasionem cognosce." At Scott's suggestion, this Latin version of "an opportunity for learning" became the title.

Later, Moore replaced it with "I've Been Thinking," formerly the first line of the poem.

At about the same time, Moore retyped the poem with a new title, " 'Avec Ardeur,' " a borrowing from an amusing poem by Mme. de Bouffleurs, the eighteenth-century wit. The French poem appears among Moore's own, printed as a footnote to "Tom Fool at Jamaica."

As the new dedication to "Avec Ardeur" makes clear, Moore had in mind while composing her poem Ezra Pound both as translator (he had published a translation of the French poem) and as an important help to her with her translation of La Fontaine. The dedicatory epigraph reads: "Dear Ezra, who knows what cadence *is*." Moore sent Pound a copy of the poem and received his thanks:

> Thanks for the clarity
> & sagacity and the concern & *cadence*,
> Love from Ezra,
> You are an old man's darling!

106. Atlas canning jar marked "Atlas E-Z Seal."

107. Ezra Pound. Autograph letter signed to Marianne Moore, March 27, 1967.

108. Marianne Moore. " 'Avec Ardeur.' " Autograph manuscript, 1966. Written on front free endpaper of Marianne Moore, *Tell Me, Tell Me* (New York: Viking, 1966).

"Avec ardeur,"
    dear Ezra, who knows what cadence is.
        I've been thinking —
        I ~~mean~~ cogitating —.
            mean

: Make a fuss
and be tedious

I'm annoyed?
yes, am — I avoid

"adore"
and ~~hate~~

am, I ~~say~~
say, by
the word
bore, bores.

I refuse
to use

"divine"
to mean

something
pleasing:

"terrific color"
for some horror

Though flat myself
myself. I'd say that

"Atlas"
(pressed glass)
looks best
embossed.

I refuse
to use

"enchant"
"dement":

ever fright-
ful plight
(whenever justified)

is privat-
ive fool
(howsoever suitable)

I'm scrupled?
am still trapped

by these
word ~~diseases~~ diseases.
with ~~no~~ pauses,

the phrase

lack lyric lyric
lyric
forces unlike
~~unlike~~ Attic
please

or freak
Calico-green

(This is not secret
of course).

I'm sure of this:
Nothing mundane is divine,
Nothing divine is mundane

(Omitted by accident)
the plea

cat
dog
dog

"Old Amusement Park" 1964

A single photograph became the entire source of a poem commemorating turn-of-the-century New York. On April 16, 1964, Brendan Gill of the *New Yorker* sent Moore the photograph with an explanation:

The Port Authority sent me a press release today, about the rededication of La Guardia Airport, and among the press things was this glossy print of the old amusement park that used to stand on the site of La Guardia. Isn't it charm-

Item 109

The Gay Nineties (1892) - Gala Amusement Park, North Beach, Long Island. It later became the site of a 105-acre private flying field, the Glenn H. Curtiss Airport. The new LaGuardia Airport comprises 575 acres.

LG-3276-6404

90

ing? Why don't you write a poem about that boy leaning against the post on the curb in the left-hand margin of the picture? He has been leaning like that for seventy-two years now and doesn't look the least bit tired.

Moore replied immediately:

Producer of un"accidental Masterpieces" dear Brendan - you engender an insatiable appetite for life. How ingenious of you to illustrate what you say - always give the potent clue - the leaning boy and Pony Track. I never imagine I could please you. Ever envying you. Am keeping the picture — to use it — clue to "good writing" but if you need it, tell me.

That summer, Moore began work on the poem and the *New Yorker* published it on August 29th. Gill's suggestion had been well heeded, and the boy leaning against the post became

> A businessman, the pony-paddock boy
> locks his equestrian toy —

flags flying, fares collected,
shooting gallery neglected —
    half-official, half-sequestered,
        limber-slouched against a post,
        and tells a friend what matters least.

Despite her protestations, Moore did please Gill, and he wrote, as soon as he had seen the poem:

Oh, what a splendid poem! Will you always write a poem like that when I command it? What a sense of power it gives me, to be the occasion of bringing into the world a work of art by MM!

109. *Gala Amusement Park, North Beach, Long Island.* Copyprint of a photograph, 1962. Included in press materials distributed by the Port Authority of New York and New Jersey.

110. Brendan Gill. Autograph letter signed to Marianne Moore, April 16, 1964.

111. Marianne Moore. "Old Amusement Park." *New Yorker*, August 29, 1964, p. 34.

"In Lieu of the Lyre" 1965

"In Lieu of the Lyre" was written in April and May, 1965, for the *Harvard Advocate*. Writing to Stuart A. Davis, the student editor who requested the poem, Moore described herself: "a student, which I am — especially in debt to Harvard...." The poem conveys her gratitude to those at Harvard to whom she felt indebted, including Harry Levin, her supporter and mentor during the long process of translating *The Fables of La Fontaine*. In the poem, Moore says that the "invitation to Harvard made grateful.../one whose 'French aspect' was invented by/Professor Levin," referring, as she notes, to Harry Levin's essay in the *Festschrift for Marianne Moore's Seventy-seventh Birthday*. Her translations, of course, are Professor Levin's starting point there,

Item 112

A TRICKLE OF WATER

to which he allies her propensity for natural history. While in the debate between Nature and Art, he says, the English poets have sided with Nature and the French with Art, Moore's "dual allegiance reveals itself through a paradox: as a naturalist, Miss Moore is even more artful in her approach than Buffon." Consistent in his appraisals, Levin had referred in a 1950 Harvard symposium to Moore's "unique position as a kind of natural historian among our poets."

The lyre stands inevitably for lyric poetry. But in this instance, it also represents an engraving of a lyrebird, which Moore associated both with Harvard and with natural history in the tradition of the Comte de Buffon, the eighteenth-century pioneer in the field. The Harvard College Library had reproduced on postcards an aquatint of a lyrebird from Audebert and Vieillot's *Histoires Naturelles...des Oiseaux de Paradis.* While she was writing "In Lieu of the Lyre," Moore had a quantity of the cards and was using them for correspondence. The lyrebird, found only in Australia, was discovered in 1798 and became a favored subject of illustrators of natural history. Not only has the male of the species an elegant lyre-shaped tail, its song has the facility of the translator's lyre: it convincingly imitates twenty-six other species. With her propensity for the odd parallel, Moore offers in place of the lyre an engraving by Thomas Bewick, who stands in the traditions of both Buffon and La Fontaine. She knew Bewick's work well and had recently attended an exhibition of his wood engravings at New York University.

To the *Advocate*, *gratia sum*
unavoidably lame as I am, verbal
                        pilgrim
like Thomas Bewick, drinking from his
                        hat-brim,
drops spilled from a waterfall....

Item 113

This wood engraving was originally a tailpiece in Bewick's *History of British Birds* (Vol. I, Land Birds, 1797), which, with his *Water Birds* and *Quadrupeds*, form his landmark contribution to natural history. Although the major engravings in the book are those of birds, small rural scenes, often depicting Bewick himself, decorate the ends of chapters. Here, in a tailpiece called "A Trickle of Water," Bewick pictures himself drinking water from his hatbrim. Moore's own reference for the tailpiece was the *Memoir of Thomas Bewick*, a 1961 reprint by the Centaur Press, which she had obtained on March 26, 1965. In this edition, the tailpiece on page 53 follows the chapter in which Bewick describes his first success, the reception of his engravings done for Aesop's *Fables*, and his gratitude for the prize he won for them. Included in the picture is a heart-shaped carving on a rock, above which is written "gratia sum," Bewick's thanks for a refreshing waterfall and for his success.

There is further evidence that Moore associated Bewick with her own *Fables of La Fontaine*. The "gratia sum" tailpiece was reproduced on the title page of *Thomas Bewick: A Resume of His Life and Work* by Graham Reynolds (London, 1949), which Moore received from Mrs. W. Murray Crane in January 1950. Deeply engaged in her translations, Moore paid particular attention to comments about *Aesop's Fables*, which Bewick illustrated in 1784 and again in 1818, his first and last major works. In particular, Moore marked the following passage:

> In the Fables of Aesop and Others, 1818, Bewick puts himself into the genealogical tree of fable writers by cutting a vignette over the introduction, a stone on which is written the line of his forebears, beginning with Jonathan and David, proceeding through Aesop to La Fontaine, L'Estrange, de la Motte, Gay, Croxall, Moore, Draper, Didsley, and Brook Boothby.

Like Bewick, Moore knew the value of aid in work on fables, and in choosing his "gratia sum" to express her thanks, acknowledged her forebears with a vignette.

112. Thomas Bewick. "A Trickle of Water." *Memoir of Thomas Bewick*. New York: Centaur Press, 1961, p. 53.

113. Jean-Baptiste Audebert and Louis Jean-Pierre Vieillot. *The Lyre Bird*. Postcard, n.d. Reproduced from *Histoires Naturelles...des Oiseaux de Paradis* (Paris, 1802).

114. Antonio Callado. "Literary Letter from Brazil." *The New York Times Book Review*, January 4, 1953, p. 14.

115. Marianne Moore. "In Lieu of the Lyre." *The Harvard Advocate*, November 1965, p. 5.

"The Camperdown Elm" 1967

Marianne Moore was appointed president of the Greensward Foundation in 1965 and for the next several years pursued the Foundation's goals: to foster and promote public appreciation of Central and Prospect Parks (in New York and Brooklyn) and other parks designed by Frederick Law Olmstead; to contribute to their restoration and beautification; to encourage research about them; and to collect and preserve drawings, plans, paintings, books, and other records about them. Her activities included making a plea for budget allocations at City Hall, writing the introduction to Clay Lancaster's *Prospect Park Handbook* (1967), and helping to save the Camperdown elm with a poem.

Prospect Park's Camperdown elm, planted in 1872, was found in 1966 to be endangered by rot. Marie M. Graff, horticultural consultant to the park, prepared a leaflet to help raise $500 toward restoring it to health. From the leaflet Moore took suggestions for the tree's "intricate branch pattern" and the treatment applied by the Bartlett Tree Expert Company specialist. For comparison, Moore turned to an elm in Manhattan, that in Asher B. Durand's painting, "Kindred Spirits," at the New York Public Library. Durand shows William Cullen Bryant in conversation with Thomas Cole.

When the poem first appeared, the Hudson River School painter's name was written as

Item 116

PROSPECT PARK'S CAMPERDOWN ELM TODAY. WILL IT BE ALIVE IN 1972?

95

"Timothy Cole." Within a week, letters arrived to explain that Timothy Cole (1853-1931), an engraver, was the wrong artist. Moore, who did know her Cole, made the correction in the second impression of *Complete Poems*. Named for the last line in Keats's sonnet "O Solitude! If I must with thee dwell," the painting hung above a bench outside the library's main reading room, a spot often chosen by Moore for quiet conversation.

116. *The Camperdown Elm, Prospect Park's Chief Treasure since 1872.* New York: Friends of Prospect Park, [*circa* 1966].

117. Jacques Hnizdovsky. *Camperdown Elm, Pros-* *pect Park.* Greeting card. New York: Friends of Prospect Park, [*circa* 1966]. The cards were sold to raise funds for restoring the tree.

118. *Bartlett Tree Expert Company Tree Surgeon with His Arm inside the Camperdown Elm.* Photograph, [*circa* 1966].

119. Asher B. Durand. *Kindred Spirits.* Oil on canvas, 1849. Reproduction, n.d. The original hangs in the New York Public Library. Lenox Astor Tilden Foundations.

120. Marianne Moore. "The Camperdown Elm." *Complete Poems.* New York: Macmillan/ Viking, 1981, p. 242.

Item 117

Item 119

"Tippoo's Tiger" 1967

Moore derived "Tippoo's Tiger," as she stated in her note to the poem, from a Victoria & Albert Museum monograph. This illustrated booklet was given to her by Lincoln Kirstein in 1963, and her characteristic marginal markings adorn nearly every page. What those markings show is that "derived" is the apt word: every line in the poem quotes from or summarizes material in the monograph.

"Tippoo's Tiger" is a wooden construction nearly six feet long and two and a half feet high which depicts a prostrate European being savaged

Item 122

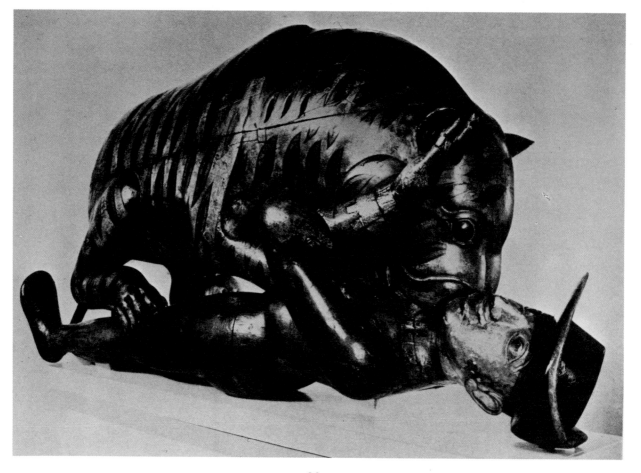

by a Bengal tiger. Inside is a wooden pipe organ operated by a handle inserted into the tiger's chest. When the handle is cranked, the victim's forearm waves and the organ emits sounds "very much like the growling cough of the Bengal tiger at its kill." To explain the origin of the man-tiger-organ, the "vast toy" and "curious automaton," Mildred Archer presents the history of Tipu Sultan, ruler of Mysore, India, killed in a battle with British troops in 1799. Tipu, or Tippoo, had been named for the tiger and took the beast as his symbol with the device, "The Lion of God is the Conqueror" (lion and tiger are both "tipu" in the Sultan's language, Canarese). His favorite form of hunting most evidenced his "tigerish qualities": he trained cheetahs to hunt antelope. During Tipu's reign, the only son of Sir Hector Monro fell victim to a tiger on Sauger Island, and was carried off and fatally mauled before his companions could shoot the beast.

The story of this event made its way back to England where it became a popular subject for potters and carvers. Archer details in objective fashion the story of Tipu as it relates to the man-tiger-organ. Moore extracted from the monograph only material related to Tipu as tiger — with one exception, the description of the carpet taken from Keats's "Cap and Bells." She relegates the organ itself to the end of the poem, emphasizing instead Tipu's delusion "that his war was holy / and that a tiger is a deity." Her story becomes one of compound losses by Tipu and the British summed up by the outrageous artifact, the man-tiger-organ.

In support of the story of Tipu's losses, Moore took one ingredient from Archer's report, that Tipu trained cheetahs to hunt antelope. To it she added, as if it were part of Tipu's own experience, Saki's tale about the polecat ferret, joining fact and fiction to make Tipu suffer a loss not his but one invented by the relative of his enemy. In turn, the loss becomes a precursor of Tipu's fate.

The infidel claimed Tipu's helmet and cuirasse
and a vast toy, a curious automaton —
a man killed by a tiger; with organ pipes inside
from which blood-curdling cries merged
        with inhuman groans.
The tiger moved its tail as the man moved
        his arm.

121. Mildred Archer. *Tippoo's Tiger*. London: The Victoria and Albert Museum, 1959.

122. *Tippoo's Tiger*. Painted wood with metal fixtures. Seringapatam, Mysore, India, [*circa*, 1795]. In the collections of The Victoria and Albert Museum, London. Postcard, n.d.

123. Marianne Moore. *Tippoo's Tiger*. New York: The Phoenix Book Shop, 1967.

"The Magician's Retreat" 1970

A small color reproduction of René Magritte's painting *Domain of Lights* from *The New York Times Magazine* suggested the images in "The Magician's Retreat." The Magritte picture portrays a house among dark trees, lit by a lamppost, all set against a bright noonday sky. It reveals, in Moore's description, a house

> cloudy but bright inside
> like a moonstone,
> while a yellow glow
> from a shutter-crack shone,
> and a blue glow from the lamppost
> close to the front door.

The surreal quality of the painting is reinforced by the title of the poem. Moore had a copy of *Arts Magazine* which carried an article about the work of an eighteenth-century visionary architect, Jean-Jacques Lequeu. On the cover appeared *Repaire des magiciens*, or "The Magicians' Retreat," an eerie architectural drawing of a gothic house. Niches with magicians in pointed hats and elephant gargoyles ornament the facade. Moore took the title of this drawing and wrote it at the top of her clipping showing Magritte's painting, renaming it for her poem.

124. René Magritte. *Domain of Lights*. Oil on canvas, 1953-54. In the collections of The Peggy Guggenheim Foundation, Venice. Reproduction published in *The New York Times Magazine*, January 19, 1969, p. 69.

125. Jean-Jacques Lequeu. *Repaire des magiciens*. Drawing, n.d. Reproduced in *Arts Magazine*, December/January 1967/68, cover illustration.

126. Marianne Moore. "The Magician's Retreat." *Complete Poems*. New York: Macmillan/Viking, 1981, p. 246.

Item 124

RENÉ MAGRITTE: "Domain of Lights," 1953-54.
The contrast between a noonday sky and a nighttime silhouette of trees and a house gives a supernatural effect to this work by Belgium's leading surrealist.

arts magazine

DECEMBER/JANUARY 1968   **$1.25**

in this issue: visionary architects . lawrence alloway on marilyn monroe . the fictionalization of the past . dore ashton on fashions . posters

"Prevalent at One Time" 1970

PREVALENT AT ONE TIME

I've always wanted a gig
semi-circular like a fig
for a very fast horse with long tail
for one person, of course;

and then a tiger-skin rug,
for my Japanese pug,
the whole thing glossy black.
I'm no hypochondriac.

The last poem Marianne Moore wrote draws upon a history of Greenwich Village, the site of her first and last homes in New York. The "gig" which she "always wanted" is pictured in *New York's Greenwich Village* by Edmund T. Delaney in an engraving from about 1850. The illustration shows the street in front of 235 Broadway where a high-stepping horse is pulling a small semicircular carriage, a little black dog chasing along behind.

The image of a gourd-shaped gig goes back to an illustration, probably for a children's story, in which three rats sail a boat made from a gourd. On the back of the picture is a note from Moore to her brother, sending him the picture "courtesies of the gig." For years, this picture was kept in a small wallet with Moore's favorite photographs of her mother and brother. The fanciful rats suggest the Moore family, since Marianne was called "Rat" by her mother and brother, after the poet in *The Wind in the Willows*.

Item 127

102

127. *235 Broadway.* Engraving, n.d. Reproduction published in Edmund T. Delaney, *New York's Greenwich Village* (Barre, Massachusetts: Barre Publishers, 1968), p. 54.

128. *Three Rats Sailing a Gourd-boat.* Mounted clipping from a magazine, n.d. Inscribed by Marianne Moore December 25, 1926.

129. *Captain John Warner Moore with Chief Leato.* Photograph, June 1933.

130. *Marianne Moore and Her Mother, Mary Warner Moore, in Cummington, Massachusetts.* Photograph, 1942.

131. Marianne Moore. *Prevalent at One Time.* Philadelphia: Privately printed, 1970.

Items 128-130

103

This catalogue
has been designed and printed
by Cypher Press, Inc.
The type has been set in California
by Graphitype
and is printed on Tapestry Cover
and Finch Opaque text